Agile Readiness

This book is dedicated to my dear wife Nance, and my children.
It is their support, dedication and encouragement through the years of my
education, teaching, long hours and late nights, and early mornings that
makes this work possible. I want to thank you all, and hope that each of you
may be encouraged as you work toward your dreams.
Thank you. Love, Tom.

This book is dedicated to my Savior, Jesus Christ, my sweet wife Pauline, and
my children Chrislyn, Jayden and Ethan. Their unconditional love is truly an
inspiration. My parents, Baskaran Daniel and Nirmala Daniel, need a special
mention since they taught me to crawl, walk and run.
Thank you. Love, Reuben.

Agile Readiness

Four Spheres of Lean and Agile Transformation

THOMAS P. WISE
and
REUBEN DANIEL

GOWER

Published by
Gower Publishing Limited
Wey Court East
Union Road
Farnham
Surrey, GU9 7PT
England

Gower Publishing Company
110 Cherry Street
Suite 3-1
Burlington, VT 05401-3818
USA

www.gowerpublishing.com

British Library Cataloguing in Publication Data
A catalogue record for this book is available from the British Library

ISBN: 978 1 4724 1743 5 (hbk)
ISBN: 978 1 4724 1744 2 (ebk – ePDF)
ISBN: 978 1 4724 1745 9 (ebk – ePUB)

Library of Congress Cataloging-in-Publication Data
Wise, Thomas P.
  Agile readiness : four spheres of lean and agile transformation / by Thomas P. Wise and Reuben Daniel.
      pages cm
  Includes bibliographical references and index.
  ISBN 978-1-4724-1743-5 (hbk) -- ISBN 978-1-4724-1744-2 (ebook) --
  ISBN 978-1-4724-1745-9 (epub) 1. Organizational change. 2. Teams in the workplace.
  3. New products--Management. 4. Computer software--Development. I. Daniel, Reuben.
  II. Title.
  HD58.7.W574 2015
  658.4'013--dc23
                                                                        2014029832

Printed in the United Kingdom by Henry Ling Limited,
at the Dorset Press, Dorchester, DT1 1HD

Contents

List of Figures and Table   *vii*

About the Authors   *ix*

Foreword   *xi*

Acknowledgements   *xvii*

Introduction: As an Executive, What Do I Need?   1

1   Who's Eating Your Lunch?   9

2   Myths and Common Pitfalls   15

3   Individual Behaviors That Enable   53

4   Team Roles and Responsibility   79

5   Management Governance: Process in Support of Agile
        and Lean Readiness   93

6   Organizational Institutionalization   129

7   Lean Manufacturing: A Case in Study   147

Bibliography   *165*

Index   *175*

List of Figures and Table

Figures

I.1	Four spheres of agile and lean transformation	2
I.2	Laying the foundation	4
2.1	Trend analysis of word searches from 2005 to 2014	16
2.2	Levers that improve agility	37
2.3	Communication options	48
5.1	The need for process transformation	96
5.2	Benefits of an agile transformation	96
5.3	Relationship between agile and lean	101
5.4	Heat maps provide immediate visual indication of strength and weakness	102
5.5	Project complexity and governance	104
5.6	Four quadrant project chartering guide	107
5.7	Solutions need to account for the customer	108
6.1	Lean and agile are complimentary	139
6.2	Lean readiness categories	142
6.3	Agile readiness survey results	143

Table

2.1	Distribution of successful agile and lean implementation in retrospective data	21

About the Authors

Dr Thomas P. Wise has a Ph.D. in Organizational Management from Capella University with specialization in Information Technology Management currently teaching part-time at Villanova University in the MS Engineering Computer Science program, and part-time with the DeSales University in the MBA and MSIS programs. His previous books include *Trust in Virtual Teams* with Gower Publishing and a couple of works of fiction. As Director of Quality Management for a major communications company, Dr Wise is responsible for process improvement, problem-solving, internal consulting and assessments, as well as quality assurance and metrics and reporting at the National Engineering and Technical Operations National Test Lab in Pennsylvania, USA.

Dr Wise is a member in good standing with the American Society for Quality (ASQ) in Millwaukee, Wisconsin, USA, and an ASQ certified Manager of Quality and Organizational Excellence since 1997. Wise is also a certified Management Professional (since 1998) with the Project Management Institute Project located in Newtown Square Pennsylvania, USA. His education includes a BS Organizational Management and a dual major in Human Resource Management from the College of St. Francis, Joliet, Illinois, USA, and a Master's in Business Administration specialized in management from the University of St. Francis, Joliet, Illinois. The author's work experience includes work as an internal quality consultant with a major commercial nuclear power electric production company, and the development of quality programs for major financial market producers. Dr Wise currently resides in the Philadelphia, Pennsylvania area with his family.

As a quality professional in the industries of commercial nuclear, financial, and mass media, experiences in project and quality management have led to an interest in project, software and systems development, and quality, and the effect these processes have on the human interests of trust and communication. Of particular interest, and current research, is understanding the effect of a virtual work environment in the areas of project, systems and software development, and quality management has upon trust and communication. Current research includes trust in virtual project teams in relation to the variable employee role and the elements of virtuality.

Reuben Daniel is an engineer and an MBA with specialization in Information Systems currently working as a Director of Business Consulting focusing on Communications and Technology industries at Cognizant Technology Solutions. As a Business Consulting leader, Reuben is an expert in process transformations, business performance management, innovation, organizational change and business – technology alignment.

Reuben has earned certifications in Lean, Six Sigma, Agile, CMMi, ITIL, CISA, ISO 20000 and ISO 9000. His education includes a Bachelor's in Engineering specializing in Metallurgical Engineering from the National Institute for Technology, India, and a Master's in Business Administration specialized in Information Systems from Anna University, India. His practical experience includes work as Business-Technology process consultant across various industries including Banking and Financial services, Insurance, Healthcare and Communications. Reuben currently resides in Central Jersey, USA with his family.

As a management consulting professional Reuben has focused much of his work on business process transformations and process change. He has handled several major clients across several industries in his 15-year stint at Cognizant. He has presented in several forums and conferences including a few key ones, such as "Enabling organizations to drive their objectives using Lean and Agile" at tmforum World Conference 2014, "Business Process Transformations that are truly Agile" at tmforum World Conference 2012, "Return on Investment for Process Improvements" at Software Engineering Process Group North America Conference, "Reducing Cost of Quality" at Software Engineering Process Group Asia, "Automating Quality" at Software Engineering Process Group Asia (that won the "Best of the Best" practices award).

He is currently leading the global business process transformation line of business for Communications industry vertical at Cognizant Technology Solutions and is also the Consulting and Innovation partner for a major telecommunications giant.

Foreword

Over the years, many companies have launched Agile and Lean initiatives with the objective of reducing complexity and waste, and ultimately saving money. Many of the same companies have also executed large business and IT transformation programs where they implemented new processes and/or technologies, such as ERP, CRM, etc. Typically these two different types of initiatives are run in very different ways, by different teams, and with different executive sponsors. They are often disconnected, rarely overlapping or interacting even though they coexist many times in the same unit of a company.

What *Agile Readiness* does is ask the critical questions on whether we can increase the success rate and value of the Agile or Lean initiatives by applying some of the same thinking and methodologies that make business and IT transformations a success by utilizing key elements of organizational change management.

There are several *common challenges* and pitfalls that should be looked for in any Agile and Lean implementation, such as:

- Inappropriately structured program governance that does not consider all key stakeholders and neglects the need for oversight and clear decision making at the right level.

- Insufficient consideration of the specific needs, requirements and cultures for delivery within the countries and regions where deployment will take place.

- Poorly planned and executed mobilization and alignment building early on in the program.

- A lack of visibility into the risks, issues and dependencies at a program level.

- Benefit realization not being tracked at a Program Level resulting in scope creep and inadequate capturing of value from the program.

The authors explain how the journey to a Lean or Agile initiative begins with proactively identifying challenges, exploring their root causes, leading to strategic solutions and behavioral changes to prevent them in the future. The process changes that accompany the Lean or Agile implementations require a focus at the business level rather than at the personnel level, as the problems are bigger than the practitioner.

This book explains the four critical ingredients for success of any Lean or Agile implementation:

1. *Individual Behavior*: focuses on the core behaviors at the individual level.

2. *Team Roles and Responsibility*: clearly defined roles and responsibilities.

3. *Management Governance*: team governance strategy and guidelines for decision-making and prioritization.

4. *Organizational Institutionalization*: making the change stick via clear change vision, communications and leadership support and commitment throughout the process.

The authors go on to explain why copying successful Agile/Lean transformation approaches from other businesses, and then expecting great success in their own organization, is a method that does not always work. They dispel the myth that assumes transformation can be accomplished with some degree of success by lifting the practices of one company, or group, and dropping them into an unrelated group or company.

One of the critical pillars of a successful Agile/Lean transformation is changing individual behaviors and leadership. The changes associated with transformation programs, if not managed appropriately, will present several challenges for the program team to overcome. These challenges will likely include:

- Ensuring executives and business leaders are fully aligned and committed to the program – and are actively participating in the program governance structure.

- Defining business priorities, along with any unique operating requirements across diverse global regions, and identifying opportunities to harmonize and/or incorporate into the global solution.

- Estimating and articulating business benefits in a manner that resonates with key stakeholders, employees and influences commitment – and then working with those stakeholders to ensure those benefits are realized.

- Articulating a compelling vision for the change, one that can be consistently communicated and readily internalized and accepted across the impacted areas.

- Providing the "right-fit" resources that will ensure appropriate involvement and input to the strategy/plan and work activities.

- Establishing an aggressive timeline that will enable the program to achieve value realization targets – yet ensure appropriate cadence to bring along the organization without unnecessary business disruption.

A robust Organizational Change Management framework is a must to make these types of projects successful and incorporates eight key elements that address these transformational challenges and successfully enable changes globally:

1. *Change Strategy*: Sets the overarching strategy for managing the change, including establishing the case for change and project governance structure.

2. *Impact Identification and Readiness*: Identifies how each affected audience will be impacted by the project changes, and tracks their progression towards readiness.

3. *Stakeholder Engagement*: Identifies the affected stakeholders of a project, and develops a framework and plan for engaging and aligning leadership members.

4. *Communications*: Engages affected stakeholder groups to prepare them for the coming changes, including planning, development, and delivery of messages.

5.   *Benefits Realization*: Defines what project success looks like, and builds a framework for assigning accountability and tracking Key Performance Indicators.

6.   *Organization Design*: Determines how an organization's design (for example, departments, reporting hierarchy, job definitions) should transition during a change.

7.   *Learning and Development*: Prepares end users to successfully perform their job using the new business processes, including completing tasks in the new system.

8.   *Culture*: Assesses the elements that drive an organization's culture, and determines how those elements can drive strategic improvements.

I have always said the "soft stuff" is the hard stuff and many initiatives fail to deliver the results and properly motivate people to adopt changes because proper change management best practices are never adopted as part of the program. We have seen too many times that mandating changing and using a "2 by 4" mentality with the associates will ensure the delivery of suboptimal results.

In my experience, Agile and Lean initiatives suffer from the same challenges as other types of business & IT transformation programs. In many instances, they fail to accomplish the goals that were set out at the beginning and/or they slowly lose momentum as management turns its attention to newer priorities. By applying these proven transformation and change management approaches to Agile and Lean initiatives, as the authors are proposing, companies can avoid many common pitfalls to realize and sustain the value these initiatives promise.

The authors conclude the book by sharing one of the most important tenets of success in any Agile or Lean transformation program. It is the risk taking capability of the organization and its people which makes a difference as they embark on an Agile/Lean journey. In any Agile/Lean transformation program, employees need to feel they have the allowance of small failures as they come to grips with their new skills and responsibilities. As in every new endeavor, people have to take a risk as they step up to learn new skills and behaviors, and risk-taking requires the acceptance that failure is inevitable until the new skills become engrained in the way work gets done.

I am convinced that this important and timely book will help many leaders with getting more value from their Lean and Agile initiatives and in doing so will move the rate of adoption up for these valuable types of programs across the corporate world.

Mark G. Livingston
Executive Vice President, Cognizant Business Consulting Global Practice Leader
Cognizant Technology Solutions

Acknowledgements

All of those who are cited here in, and those whose research guided our experiences and education as we drew upon their knowledge in our work should be acknowledged for their contribution. Those with whom we work are given our thanks for their patient understanding as we practiced what we preached.

This book represents many years of learning and research, both secondary and primary, and the experiences as an internal consultant and line manager in many of the practices in organizational, IT, and product quality, and years of knowledge gathering in business and process improvement consultation.

We would like to especially note, and thank, Janai Wise for her work, and her guidance on the illustrations and diagrams used in this book, and hope that her contribution encourages her work in professional art. I would like to acknowledge the support, love, and encouragement of my wife Nance, and my children for their smiles, hugs, and enthusiasm for this project. You have no idea how important hugs and smiles can be.

Lastly, and yet never least, we would like to acknowledge our editor, Jonathan Norman for his honest and well needed feedback, and our publication coordinator Christine Muddiman for her patient guidance.

Dr Thomas P. Wise

What started out as an idea has evolved into a book that I believe will help organizations save a lot of transformation dollars. This book is a lot more than a couple of experienced professionals sharing their stories. Support, encouragement and cheer came from my peers, leaders and friends. We would particularly like to thank Mark Livingston, EVP of Cognizant Business Consulting, and Charles Goldenberg, Todd Weinert and Shameka Young of Cognizant Business Consulting, for their kind words of encouragement. Special thanks to Naresh Nirmal, of Cognizant Business Consulting, for helping to edit the book. We are grateful to Adrian O'Leary, Clarence Mitchell and Arbela Takhsh for being inspiring leaders.

This section is incomplete without special acknowledgement to the talented co-author, Dr Thomas P. Wise. He transformed ideas into powerful business solutions.

Reuben Daniel

Introduction

As an Executive, What Do I Need?

It is always a challenge to write in words all that management may need, or that which management should consider when it comes to implementing Agile and Lean. As Organizational Change practitioners, we have seen implementations fall well short of their intended goals, or in some cases continue to stutter along aimlessly and with little hope as their leaders struggle to maintain a positive outlook for success. In hopes of sparing many of you the same pain and suffering we have experienced over the years, this book primarily addresses two key questions:

- Is the agile and lean implementation well positioned for success?

- What are the essential levers I need to move to maximize the chances of the program to meet its proposed goals?

This book is not a beginner text on agile or lean frameworks, as it will not answer the question regarding a concise "How to" practitioner guide to agile or lean. Nor is it about how to get the basics up and running. We assume you have the basic idea and awareness of these methodologies and are likely well versed in the basic methods of agile and lean practice. It is also not our intention to convince you to implement agile and lean methodologies. We suggest that you consult a competent agile coach or a Lean Master Black Belt if you need to know if agile or lean is right for you. This book is for the executives that desire to ensure their organization is well positioned to successfully implement an agile program or lean waste reduction. This book is also for the program sponsors and is expected to be a guide on behaviors, strategies, and processes critical to agile and lean business transformation. This book presents to our readers the "Four Spheres Model of Agile and Lean Transformation," so it is strongly recommended that you read this introductory chapter prior to reading other parts of this book.

The four spheres of agile and lean transformation, as depicted in Figure I.1, are a simple model by which a practitioner may prepare their organizations for agile and lean implementation in a way that will help organizations realize benefits. The four spheres are intended to be the "Step 0," or the required foundation, before an organization launches a major Agile/Lean initiative. For most organizations that are already well into their implementations, or firms that are flirting with these process methods, the four spheres will provide the right reference point to fill in the gaps to improve their chances of success.

Individual Behavior, in Chapter 3, is the anchor for agile and lean, and therefore where the model begins; with a solid core built upon the behaviors of the individual. We can all agree as leaders and managers that proper behavior is key. It gives the team their mass that when combined with a clearly directed vision, the acceleration that gives true force to the effort. Proper behaviors are what maintain the flight when adversity strikes like a golf iron, ripping the team out of the rough when a path correction is necessary, and gives long flight with a narrow path on a daily basis. The core behaviors are what keep the organization formed into a cohesive,

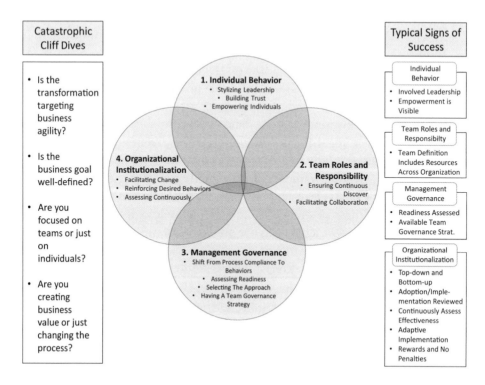

Figure I.1   Four spheres of agile and lean transformation

functioning, and effective force. It is the attitude that make the can-do "way" into a got it done philosophy.

Chapter 4 details the team roles and responsibilities that form the wrapper within which the core behaviors are able to form a cloak of kinship and give shape to a team. In effectively developing team roles the individuals can form relationships that both support their individual skills and desires within the organization, and develop a structure within which the individuals may find membership. Clearly defined and unique roles provide individuals the ability to understand how they fit into the vision and mission, how their skills, their energy, their strengths and weaknesses connect with one another.

In Chapter 5, Management Governance provides the path upon which the teams travel. It prevents wandering and eliminates the roadblocks, levels the ruts cut in the road that led to past successes, and soothes the cuts and bruises that accumulate as the team works through the battles that inevitably come when new ways of getting work done are adopted. Reinforcing new behaviors is essential to making the shift from a traditional life cycle, and prerequisite in the process of maturing in the new methods and organizational norms.

Making it stick, otherwise known as Organizational Institutionalization in Chapter 6, is often where an organization falls down in the transformation process. In this the most outer sphere and the wrapper that makes everything worth the effort the leaders of the organization must provide a continuous stream of communication. Everyone needs to be aware of the change. The whole of the organization, from the "shop floor" to the "ivory tower" must have the vision and the mission in their windshield and a clear view of the past efforts to share in the celebration of small wins and the anticipation of forthcoming victories.

We have chosen to begin at a point in which laying the foundation will make sense (see Figure I.2). Chapter 2 jumps right into the failures and traps of agile and lean methods and the practices that may drive your program into the ditch, and so we choose to begin with establishing a common language and vision for the future that may indeed help you to avoid a few of those pitfalls as we proceed. It is to ensure that we have a common understanding of terms. Jargon is everywhere in the world of business transformation, and these terms may refer to several different concepts for different readers in different industries. Common definitions are critical, not just for you as a reader, but also for your transformation program.

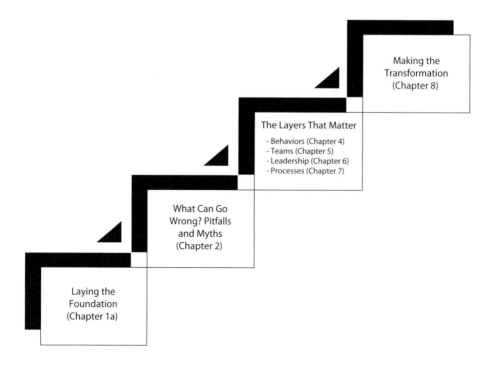

Figure I.2   Laying the foundation

Jargon is the enemy of the common vision and mission. We never forget our early experiences, and in a conversation recently an associate was reminded of his days as a technical writer in the nuclear power industry. This is an industry that prides itself on a common mission and an understanding of the details that would make even a seasoned practitioner blush. As a writer he had spent many weeks agonizing over every word in my report to ensure the perfect sentence was crafted throughout my detailed 3,000-word white paper on the virtues of shared responsibility. He proudly carried the report to the quality assurance reviewer and settled it neatly on the desk of the QA manager and retreated to await the praise. He described the situation as feeling aghast and shame as he received, the very next day, a harsh and critical response, something to the effect of "What in the name of Sam Hill have you done?" We do hope you don't mind the use of an old eighteenth-century American euphemism that precludes the use of more colorful language.

In effect, the seasoned quality assurance reviewer had found the paper to be so saturated with nuclear industry jargon as to make the paper unreadable to even the most seasoned of nuclear professionals. He had failed to make the author understand due to the overuse of normally acceptable and understandable industry terminology. The terminology, he sadly discovered, was found to be used differently and uniquely for several of our internal departments. It is often the case that implementations struggle because the teams do not have consistent definitions of these approaches.

The next chapter describes why we are here, and the following chapter provides insights on common pitfalls and cliff dives of agile and lean transformations designed to help the most seasoned executive set the path straight for even the most ardent supporter of agile and lean implementations. Several widespread and common myths, mostly created by ignorance and lack of experience, complicate the transformation program. To employ another common American euphemism, this chapter will help you avoid the alligators in the sewer and is most suited for organizational leaders who have some experience leading some form of agile and lean program.

The final chapter is focused on helping organizations determine their readiness for agile and lean. Establishing the organizational readiness in terms of process, training, support, and vision is an essential prerequisite prior to the launch of such transformations. Having a complete view of the organization's ability to thrive upon the launch of your agile and lean program is an essential factor in ensuring a successful launch and institutionalization of the new program. Yet more important is the ability to make an assessment and redirect a program that is struggling and already underway. A proven approach to measure and improve readiness is provided.

What is Lean?

The twenty-first century business context pleads for any strategic program to be scalable, and lean is no exception. The best definition for lean in the industry is provided by Craig Larman and Bas Vodde, authors of *Scaling Lean and Agile Development*. Lean, or lean thinking, is the English name popularized by MIT researchers to describe the system now known as the Toyota Way inside the company that created it. The essence of lean is that each individual employee is given the opportunity to find problems in his own way of working, to solve them and to make improvements. Typically lean is considered as a repository of methods like one-piece flow, kanban, and other lean tools. But experience and understanding business value reveal that lean thinking is a committed management investing in their people at all levels to promote a culture of continuous improvements, measured and validated by the customer.

What is Agile?

In a similar note, the best scalable agile model is defined by Dean Leffingwell in his several publications. The Scaled Agile Framework (SAFe), developed by Dean and other contributors, describes an organizational, process and requirements model for implementing agile methods at enterprise scale. This agile framework and the related terminology mentioned in this book are essentially IT focused and software-development centric.

At the project level, agile teams of seven team members, give or take a couple of team members depending on the needs of the team and project goals, define, build, and test user stories in a series of iterations and release increments. In the smallest enterprise, there may be only a few such teams. In larger enterprises "Pods" of such teams work together to build value streams, be they a feature, component, product in a product suite, application, subsystem or whatever. At the program level, development of larger scale systems functionality is accomplished via multiple teams in a synchronized "Agile Release Train" model described as a standard cadence of time-boxed iterations and releases that are date fixed and quality fixed, but scope variable. At the portfolio management level, a mix of investment themes, that are used to drive the investment priorities for the enterprise, are managed. That construct is used to assure that the work being performed is the work necessary for the enterprise to deliver on its chosen business strategy.

What is Transformation?

Let us start by determining what transformation is not. It is not agile or lean implementation. It is not process change or driving automation initiatives. John P. Kotter defines the goal of transformation: to make fundamental changes in how business is conducted in order to help cope with a new, more challenging market environment. It can be more specifically stated as changes made to the business to increase customer experience or value.

How is Six Sigma Differentiated from Lean?

Lean thinking reduces waste and increases customer value. Six Sigma approaches the subject of change, or problem-solving in a broader sense, and focuses on reducing defects. Theoretically, there are several parallels that can be drawn between these two management approaches. However, traditional

Six Sigma seems to be on the downslope in regard to utilization in the business world. Likely, much of the drop in popularity of Six Sigma is due to the need for substantial investment in the development, capture, and cataloging of process measures and metrics data for Six Sigma analysis. Such an investment in building an effective metrics suite is mostly impractical, especially in technology and service organizations. A very close second in the popularity plunge for Six Sigma is the difficulty in adaptable practices for technology processes. With technology highly dependent upon thought workers, the means by which one may quantify work challenges even the best of Six Sigma practitioners. Thirdly the belt structure (Yellow, Green, and Black) makes the process extremely hierarchical in an environment in which flat structures and the freedom to roam and create are the mantra. Self-expression is cherished among technology workers, and in a hierarchical methodology such as Six Sigma where a line staff member does not have the ability to execute a process improvement, if he or she is not a black belt, this fundamentally conflicts with most technology departments. Fourthly, from the traditional bottom-up implementation strategy employed in most Six Sigma programs, only incremental changes are triggered and breakthrough radical improvements are rare. It does not effectively interlace with the organizational innovation process.

For the above reasons, we are not using Six Sigma and lean thinking interchangeably. Unless otherwise stated, the focus is on lean thinking only. This book provides an essential pre-requisite to major agile or lean transformation initiatives. It can also be used as a powerful diagnostic tool for ongoing programs. There are several different methodologies in the industry today. The creative technologist is packaging more solutions into generic methods and approaches every passing day. Agile, Lean, Six Sigma, are evolving its shape as businesses are pushing for agility and efficiency. The rise in popularity of Dev Ops is just around the corner. However, this book will convince you that the four spheres model is fundamental and is applicable, independent of the transformation methodology.

Chapter 1
Who's Eating Your Lunch?

The little guys are eating our lunch, and there doesn't seem to be a thing we can do about it.

They're quick, agile, and run lean. Lunch eaters like them sprint their way around us, the 300-pound gorilla in the market, while we pretend it isn't happening, not willing to address this nimble little irritant. We try not to notice that the nimble little lunch eaters have grown, packing on pachyderm-size pounds, becoming the great white elephant in the room that we try to ignore while they feast, and we waste away, longing for our lunch. New products seem to flow from their creative engine and stream into the market place, and for them it works. They poach our customers, picking off the early adopters, the tech hungry, and the dissatisfied. It's not as though we don't know what they want, the customer that is, but it takes us so long to bring our new ideas to the market that they aren't so new anymore by the time we roll them out.

These lunch eaters are often described as nimble, quick, agile. They adapt, driving new product offerings and new technologies, reshaping their processes ahead of market demands and staying just out of our reach. They run lean, not overly burdened by the same bureaucratic demands under which our large corporations toil. Lunch eaters tend to know why they exist. They see clearly the opportunities of the world around them, resolve their problems with a fine-tuned focus, and sprint toward each new product release.

How do they do it? There are stacks of books on how agile works. It's not complicated. It's not rocket science. For that matter, the processes in agile are pretty simple, straightforward, and align well with the normal practices of software development and engineering. They work well with architectural development, and business process improvement. We believe in agile and lean, because the methods work, and it works for them because they know how to be agile and have practiced how to be lean.

We've seen estimates, with a lot of glad-handing around the numbers too, that agile projects have about a 60 percent success rate (Wilson, 2011). Really? While agile practitioners point to other, more traditional methods as having less than a 50:50 shot at success, these numbers also reflect about a 40 percent failure rate for agile projects. So we wonder how successful are the 60 percentile, and what degree of success many of those firms are having with agile and lean methods. More so we wonder how an entire industry can celebrate a 40 percent failure rate.

Those that succeed must be doing something different from those that fail. Finding true failures sometimes helps in identifying ways to design success. Some of the key factors in agility-based project failures, according to Chow and Cao's 2008 study, are tied to inadequacies in leadership, trust, team work, and skill sets, as well as cultural alignment.

Successful organizations are different. Firms that successfully make the change to agile and lean methods understand that the methods of agile and lean, while well documented and widely published, require preparation before implementation. What makes agile and lean practitioners successful has less to do with their methods, and more to do with how well their leaders prepare the culture of the organization to support the methods.

Managers, as they try to make the shift to agile methods, are often left to rely upon skills developed in a command and control environment. Agility requires autonomy and the freedom to build on incremental success, and incremental success may require building upon a temporary failure. While it is common to believe that executive buy in and commitment are essential to the success of agile practices, Chow and Cao discovered the most essential factors of successful organizations have transformative leadership, well-shaped skills, and a culture of open, team-based processes and communication (2008).

We remember as we attempted to make the shift in a financial company. We had recently merged two exchanges, and were in the process of bringing our waterfall and iterative development processes in line with the agile practices of our new owner. The company gave us a coach, and a scrum framework – basic essentials of an agile process. Teams met every morning for daily sprints, planned their day, shared their goals, set their schedules, and set forth to put their plans into action. Yet the support stopped there.

Management still held to the command and control practices of a traditional development organization, and developers, testers, architects, and analysts dropped like flies. People did their level best to provide a solid, quality product; however, the ability to shift plans, change priorities, and build a network of teams was hindered. Leadership was unable to shift from person to person to ensure technology problems were identified and fixed. Demand to produce on schedule was strong, people were highly motivated to succeed in this new environment, yet fear controlled the decisions of individuals who continued to feel powerless to raise concerns. Problems remained buried as developers scrambled to meet deadlines established in the vacuum of poor communication and low levels of trust. Team members worked 18 to 20 hours per day to make up for conflicts in code design and design changes which they stumbled across during integration testing, and architects spent many sleepless nights in analysis working to adjust specifications and system designs based upon these new revelations. In the end, many strong developers left the company ahead of a mighty crash and burn during production implementation.

Lean processes and agile methods are team-based practices. Making this change requires an organization to adopt and support new organizational behaviors that support teams and new behavioral-based practices that reinforce team methods. Distributed leadership skills, communication programs designed to build trust, and problem-solving programs that help managers and team members to choose the most effective methods are essential elements in every agile and lean initiative. Leaders need the ability and tools to choose the right method for a project, whether the project is an engineering design, problem-solving initiative, process change, or product development effort.

Facing the New Leadership Challenge

Agile teams, and teams charged with defining and refining lean process improvement, face new challenges in leadership that other groups may not face. Leadership within these groups may be described as transformative and at times transient. It shifts from one person to another, or from one group to another, and potentially moves across geographic and time zones as the need for leadership with specific skills and charters shifts with project priorities. As leadership moves from person to person to accommodate the shifting priorities of the project, many of those team members taking on a leadership role take this role in addition to their day job. In a recent study, 88 percent of respondents reported taking on the leadership role of project manager while only 13 percent of the respondents reported having only one role in the project (Wise, 2013). Problems in mentoring, coaching, feedback, and skills development may become greater challenges in this setting that may hinder processes such as team dynamics, communication, trust, and problem-solving. At times, leadership may by necessity be transformative; designed to build new skills and behaviors necessary to accomplish a given task or priority. Add to the mix the need to be virtual, and leadership skills can hit the red line. Virtuality carries with it the attributes of technologically mediated communications such as IM, chat, email, text, and web-based communications using camera technologies and desktop sharing. With the addition of the virtual technologies, managers require extensive new leadership and technology skills, and the ability to draw from a vast set of communication capabilities not required in the past, as well as deep process capabilities (Wise, 2011).

We have heard executives make statements that lead us to believe they may see agile and lean as being somehow synonymous. At the same time, many may believe they are mutually exclusive practices. The reality of the situation is that they are tools, and as with any tool they must be applied to the appropriate problem. Lacking the skills in process management can be immediately apparent to a technology team, and can add to the problems leaders face (Glen, 2003).

Avoiding these problems, and building an environment ready for agility and lean is why we chose to write this book. When we talk about agile, we are talking about a culture (Kruchten, 2007), a set of methods that use as their basis for getting work done the principles and behaviors of a collective mind, a virtual team membership. Teams and virtual teams share many of the same attributes including unique roles and responsibilities, autonomy, reciprocal collaborative communications, and shared meaning. Virtual teams, however, have some attributes that are often not found in the traditional team format such as swift trust, short work-horizons, and the need for transformative and distributed leadership skills.

Agility is often described by researchers and pundits as a culture all its own, or perhaps at times a subculture within a corporate environment due to the way in which culture affects how team members perceive the behaviors and contributions of other participants. Removed from this context, agile methods become nothing more than a caricature of the culture of flexibility and creativity, and a rather poor one at that, incapable of fulfilling the purpose and former beauty it once held (Kruchten, 2007). Success, then, is dependent upon creating and maintaining a culture in which agility may flourish and grow, feeding the needs and capability of fully functioning, high-performance teams assigned to appropriate defined projects.

Lean on the other side of the equation is a philosophy of process definition, refinement, and control. Often, businesses will copy what appear to be successful solutions from other businesses and expect great success. Why not? If the solution worked for a web-great such as Google or Facebook, why would it not work just as successfully for a web-great wannabe? At times, Näslund's work tells us, this forklift mentality that assumes transformation can be accomplished with some degree of success by lifting the practices of one group and dropping them in like Microsoft add-on into an unrelated group (2008). The problem, once again, is taking a strategy or process out of the context of an agile or lean ready organization. Lean is a process for organizational improvement when the problems are not well known, and the solutions may be even less clear. In using lean we shift the internal focus of process quality to an external definition based on the desires and delight of our customer.

Each of these practices or methodologies can offer an organization great success if or when the leadership of the organization is willing and ready to lay a foundation that can facilitate the success. Taking the time to prepare the organization will provide the teams with the ability to succeed, and give the leaders the capability of transforming the processes from a linear model to one of flexibility and speed.

Chapter 2
Myths and Common Pitfalls

As international consultants there is a need to stay on top of trends and keep ahead of the curves, you may say. Normally this is not a hard a task, as businesses tend to run in packs. Where the big guys go one can be sure to find a large pack of followers that will pick up the new shiny thing, no matter the cost or casualties that may occur. Agile and lean, however, seem to be bucking that trend. The big guys picked up lean back in the 1990s, and agile became the new key word and popular phrase 10 years ago with the release of the agile manifesto. So what has driven the world to agile? The new rise of agile and lean methods in the work place is likely due to the maturing of a new crop of software and engineering students into the work place that have cut their teeth on these two methods in their university studies.

Universities all across the globe now offer classes and training in the use of agile methods in software and engineering practices. As the students graduate and entered the work place eager to express themselves and share their knowledge, they launch into new products using agile as their life cycle. This unbridled enthusiasm for the creativity and discovery they offer to their mentors allow them to drive ahead, producing new lean software packages rapidly onto the shelves for consumer use, and into the back offices of many of our top companies. These new graduates have now moved into positions of authority ramping up the usage and adoption of agile and lean methods and have contributed to the rise in the last decade. In this chapter we will discuss several of the more common problems in implementation of lean and agile, and perhaps a few potential contributors to the cause.

With the onset of the Internet age finding trends in the popularity of topics is now at our fingertips. Search engine providers such as Google offer some very nice research tools that tap into the interests of billions of people in an instant. As users search through the vast population of computers and servers across the world find information regarding their favorite topic and perhaps their new found interest, search engines store that information. Remember, nothing that crosses into the virtual world of computers ever really disappears.

Google Trends, one of the top search engine analysis tools available, provides quick insight into the interest of Internet surfers and maps the changes in their interest over time. Using this tool, we can see how interest in two or more terms compare in search results on Google over time. Pictured below in Figure 2.1 is a "search" on Google Trends on four terms: Agile, Six Sigma, Lean, and Business Process Management (BPM). Business Process Management is a management practice based on the theory that is managers focus on managing the process as a whole, that the tasks necessary to maintain process flow will function effectively. As you can see, BPM is holding its own over the past 10 years which gives credence to the interest managers have in life cycle or process effectiveness.

Six Sigma, on the other hand, has been slowly declining as a search topic, and hasn't been getting nearly as much attention as it had in 2004. Many people attribute the decline in Six Sigma popularity to the need for extensive training and the high cost of Six Sigma practitioners in the consulting world. Six Sigma Black Belts often draw six-figure incomes and quite frankly can be hard to find in the market place. Lean, a Six Sigma derivative that is light on the statistics side and easily trained and lightly mentored in practice, is holding a steady place in the search patterns of business people. Searches for agile, which many describe as being a lean method for software developers, is on the rise. Keep in mind that we are dealing with very large numbers when using search engine analysis tools.

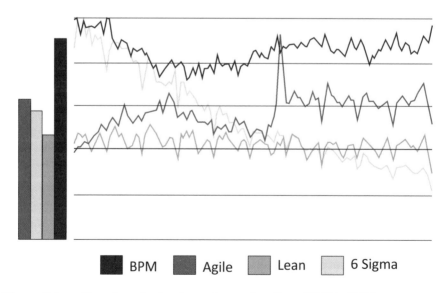

Figure 2.1   Trend analysis of word searches from 2005 to 2014

Based on the number of topic searches regarding lean and agile methods it seems apparent that organization leaders realize the value of these approaches, but may not entirely position their organization to reap the benefits. One of the leading trends in agile use is the practice of continuing to scale agile methods beyond single teams and single projects. What this means in practice is the tendency to take very complex and highly interdependent projects, often the realm of the traditional waterfall life cycle, and manage these projects using agile methods. In the year 2013 an industry survey revealed a 15 percent jump in the number of respondents who work where there are at least five agile teams, and a 9 percent increase in those working with up to five agile projects. In addition, those who plan to implement agile development in future projects have increased from 59 percent last year to 83 percent in 2013. Most, 72 percent, are using Scrum or Scrum variants as in past years.

Scrum is an iterative and incremental agile software development framework based on team membership and the incremental discovery of project information such as requirements and software architecture for managing software projects and product or application development. Kanban and Kanban variants nearly doubled this year. Kanban is a method for managing knowledge work with an emphasis on just-in-time delivery. In Kanban, as in scrum, the process is team oriented and the pace team driven in order to prevent overloading the team members with too much information. In this approach, the process, from definition of a task to its delivery to the customer, is displayed for participants to see allowing team members to pull work based on their interests and skills from a queue. For most respondents, Kanban methodologies were being applied to processes inside the software organization only (VersionOne, 2013).

Lean Shifts Quality from Fulfillment to VOC

When talking about a lean approach the consideration changes from team based decision and pacing based on the customer's defined priority to management of costs in relation to how the customer defines quality. This moves the traditional definition of quality from fulfillment of and compliance with defined requirements to the customer's priorities and definition of what is good known in some circles as the Voice of the Customer (VOC). Any manufacturing or developmental expenditure of resources that does not create value for the end customer is considered wasteful, and thus targeted for elimination.

There are several different forms of lean implementation in the industry today. There are organizations that work on a bottom-up implementation, where resources are trained, certified and then mentored to help them refine and employ their lean skills as they work on lean opportunities. This approach helps an employee perfect their lean skills and build more effective and refined processes as they improve their understanding of lean methods. Some organizational leaders like to take a more controlled and targeted implementation strategy that uses lean on a need by need basis for improving specific organizational goals, otherwise referred to as a top-down approach. Using a top-down approach helps to ensure that any changes made using lean are targeted toward the organization's strategic or tactical plans. There are also organizations that implement just the lean tools like Voice of the Customers, Value Stream Mapping, Seven QC Tools, etc. Due to having several variations in the way in which lean may be deployed in an organization, and the likelihood that an organization may simply choose to use a limited set of tools without having defined a specific lean strategy, unlike agile, lean usage statistics are often hard to collect.

It can be confidently said that most companies use one or more lean tools for waste reduction in their firms. With lean being a simplified Six Sigma strategy with the intent on focusing a company and their employees on the desires of their customers, several analysts predict that the future of lean adoption is very likely to rise. Lean principles are a perfect match for every enterprise's dilemma: creating more products, for more niches, at a faster rate and lower cost. The lean movement reaches deep into the enterprise. There are two drivers of lean principles apart from the obvious one – competitiveness. Lean has given enterprises, which have already shaved back on costs, a new language for motivating people to get creative on limited resources. Lean is appealing, then, to people in enterprise settings, particularly those who already take responsibility for agile processes. According to Shaughnessy, Brant and Patrick noted that even the owner of agile realizes their organization is not changing fast enough. That's where lean comes in (Shaughnessy, January 1, 2013).

Success Rates of Agile and Lean

Since agile and lean adoptions are on the rise, let us evaluate some of their success rates. Agile, based on a 2010 survey, is perceived to be in trouble in 45 percent of the implementations (Shaughnessy, January 1, 2013). This means that in 45 out of 100 respondents, the practitioners of agile methods believe their project is going to fail or did fail to some degree. Failure in the IT world indicates that the project did not meet the prescribed project target goals in either one or more of the categories of time, cost or quality. The failure rate quoted in the media varies widely ranging from 60 percent to 98 percent. These percentages, while they are useful to understand the general trend, become considerably more troubling when one considers that these numbers are very comparable to companies that maintained the use of the more traditional waterfall or iterative development methods. Over analyzing these percentages or comparing lean failure rates and agile success rates may not be accurate. Since lean is used both in business processes and other functions, it may not be fair to compare with agile, which is still largely software development focused, but it is quite clear that both approaches fail in many cases and as we progress in developing this chapter we intend to summarize broad pitfalls in agile and lean implementations.

There is a plethora of articles and books that focus on the challenges of agile and lean; however, most of them are largely approach and methodology driven. In most cases the authors have likely discussed organizational change as a critical challenge and the failures of managing the institutionalization of the practices of agile and lean consistently and effectively throughout the organization. In addition, factors like lack of top management support, ineffective risk mitigation and inadequate rewards and recognition are other common items on the lists. Executives and business leaders will likely see these topics as common tactical failures so prevalent in business today as to become obvious and predictable clichés. In lean parlance, these items are symptoms of deeper problems. When we take a look at these problems and explore the outcomes of failed implementations we see more than the common desire to *not rock the boat*, but rather potentially catastrophic failures in project outcomes. This chapter details a few of the key pitfalls that are potential showstoppers to the transformation initiative.

Subsequent chapters present the big picture and identify the foundational elements we perceive to be critical building blocks for these initiatives to be successful. The challenges, as we move through them and explore some of the causes, may be found to require strategic solutions and behavioral changes to prevent them in the future. The process changes that accompany the implementations require a focus at the business level rather than at the personnel level, as the problems are bigger than the practitioner. These are valuable lessons we have learned based on several years of successful and, yes, failed agile and lean implementations. We can learn as much from exploring what has failed as we can from discussing what was successful. The difference being that when focusing on the failures we learn the more valuable lesson that can only be perceived through understanding the context of the failure so to allow us to avoid these same conditions in our own implementation strategy. The need for business agility is an obvious goal statement that is emphasized in most annual reports; however, the approach taken by most organizations is not necessarily destined for success.

Over the years of travel and working with some of the largest and most successful corporations all over the world we discovered that people, like businesses, are largely the same no matter where we go. They have the same fears and desires, and likes and dislikes, for the most part. People want to be successful. People work hard and they like to be rewarded for their successes. Business leaders, after all, are people and seek the same outcomes as the rest of us – success after hard work. When working with a company on a successful or less than stellar project the information is gathered. This data is a knowledge base built up over time that collects the knowledge and learning of consultants and their experiences regarding what worked and did not work for them on their most recent project. We looked through the databases, and after analyzing the data we found a pretty clear picture of what happens in an organization as they implement lean and agile methods.

Stories from the Perspective of Practice

Within this data we found 20 organizations that recently implemented agile and lean methods in their organizations, and from this analysis we concluded some very interesting findings. The basic demographics of these 20 organizations are summarized in Table 2.1. The organizations are large corporations with more than 50,000 employees and representing four different industry verticals. Their software development organization, typically where agile was used, had at least 500 employees. We scanned through their retrospection reports hoping to find ways in which they may be similar in their implementation strategies in hope of gleaning some useful information that may help our readers avoid some of the common implementation problems. As we scanned the retrospectives a list of common problems emerged. These problems are critical pitfalls that, if we want to have a highly effective and successful implementation, we need to be bridge these issues early on:

- Equating business agility with software development agility.

- Implementing without a goal.

- Focusing on individuals not on teams.

- Focusing on process changes and not on value creation.

Table 2.1 **Distribution of successful agile and lean implementation in retrospective data**

Number of organizations	Industry	Number of organizations using agile for IT and lean for business processes	Objective success criteria defined	Number of organizations with success in transformation
6	Telecommunications	6	Yes	4
3	Banking and Financial Services	3	No	0
4	Pharmaceutical	4	No	2
4	Healthcare	4	No	I
3	Insurance	3	No	0

Equating Business Agility with Software Development Agility

Michael Hugos, author of *Business Agility* (2009: 11), summarizes the effect and need for business agility as follows:

> *The most profound innovation since the assembly line is the emergence of agile enterprise. Companies using this operative model are delivering customer value and operating profits that will become the basis for prosperity in the real-time global economy. The agile enterprise is a human driven organization whose primary assets are the relationships that exist between its employees and its customers and suppliers. It is capable of endless adaptations and reconfigurations; it evolves as its customers evolve. It is enabled by the technology it uses but is not controlled by its technology.*

With markets constantly moving and product life cycles often measured in months, companies can no longer hope to fine-tune their operations to fit some existing set of conditions and then expect simply to run those operations unchanged for years and years. This was the old business model, what history would call the industrial model. One of the greatest challenges faced by the information age is the ability to move away from the old manufacturing mindset from which the information technology industry grew, and the discovery of new and useful means by which we may define the manufacturing of information. We need something more responsive in the information age. We need something that constantly adjusts to changes and opportunities. An agile organization constantly makes many small adjustments to better respond to its changing environment. In doing so it reduces costs and increases revenue every day. No one adjustment by itself may be all that significant, but the cumulative effect of all of them over time is enormous – just like the effect of compound interest over time.

Technology, to be successfully integrated into the daily processes of any business, must be viewed as a part of business process of a company, and if used well, even as a profit center. This is a shift from technology being viewed as a back-office cost center. This point-of-view is not new, and in many cases industry has made the mental shift; however, the technology processes that are being used are still traditional. Most business agility comes from customizing existing products and services with a mix of value added services, and most value added services are information based. Mass customization is a new business trend that allows a company to provide the detailed and specific care most organizations need to compete within their area of core competency. What is valuable to one customer in a given situation is not valuable to another customer in a different situation.

The agile movement has made enormous strides in the last decade, greatly improving software delivery and the ability to deliver in a mass customization environment where the product delivery cycle is extremely short and often dependent upon the discovery process built into agile methods. Team development and self-pacing schedules inherent in agile methods have also contributed to creating more satisfactory work environments in many organizations where customization and short cycle times are the key to success. The next horizon in extending agility from basic software delivery to continuous delivery, and into the business itself utilizing the advances in delivering software features early and often, is the transformation of businesses to deliver complete solutions early and often. The drivers for this, as we will see, come from a growing focus of CEOs on trying to survive and thrive in a world of growing complexity, complication and fast moving competition.

Enterprise agility may be at a tipping point; much like agile delivery was in 2001. In 2010 IBM interviewed over 1,500 CEOs and published an in-depth study of their findings. *Capitalizing on Complexity* focused on what CEOs saw as the marketplace challenges and the key strategies for surviving and thriving in that marketplace. The IBM study revealed that CEOs are now confronted with a complexity gap, as Berman described it:

that poses a bigger challenge than any factor we've measured in eight years of CEO research. Eight in ten CEOs expect their environment to grow significantly more complex, and fewer than half believe they know how to deal with it successfully. (Berman, 2010)

Agility Is a Business Imperative

Agility is a business imperative, not just a technological one. Leaders must be ready and their organization capable of winning the advantage as opportunity arises. Opportunity is found within the changing and evolving needs of our customers or those created as shifts in technology or markets take place. Business agility, when we take into account the need being an ability to make a strategic shift or move upon an opportunity to which the practical capability may not be within the normal portfolio, is dependent upon building a core competency of flexibility in mission. When we boil this down to the area of competencies we find that agility is the ability to deal well with ambiguity and discovery, a capability in problem-solving and analysis, team development, and effective communication.

Agile software development has had great success over the past 10 years and agile project management has made inroads into the project management community, but there is a long way to go. Many companies relegate agile methods to just another in a long line of software engineering techniques while in others the transition to agile stalls after a few projects, even though those projects are successful. Too few agile transitions make an impact outside software delivery groups. What is missing? The agile movement has the potential to be absolutely strategic to businesses, particularly those whose overall strategy focuses on responsiveness over efficiency. We are selling ourselves short! We have the potential to energize new business models, engage middle and upper management in becoming agile, and change the way product and project managers connect agile concepts and practices with upper management.

Agility generates 30 percent higher profits. An overwhelming majority of executives, based on some researcher reports, greater than 80 percent, cite organizational agility as key to global success. Other studies support this idea as well. Research conducted at MIT suggests that agile firms grow revenue 37 percent faster and generate 30 percent higher profits than non-agile, yet most companies admit they are not flexible enough to compete successfully. Internal barriers stall agile change efforts (Weil, 2006). The main obstacles to improved business responsiveness are slow decision-making, conflicting departmental goals and priorities, risk-averse cultures and silo-based information. Technology can play an important supporting role in enabling organizations to become more agile companies (*The Economist* Intelligence Unit, 2009).

Lack of an effective agile model is just one part of the problem. Implementing the current models has its own misunderstandings and challenges:

> *Effectively implementing software agility at the enterprise level is no small feat. Even for the fully committed department or enterprise, it can take six months to a year to introduce and master many of the basic agile practices and a number of additional years to achieve the productivity and quality results that fully warrant the effort of such a significant enterprise-wide transformation. In Dean's discussions with teams, managers, and executives during this period, he often struggled to find a language for discussion, along with a set of abstractions and an appropriate graphic that he could use to quickly describe "what your enterprise would look like after such an agile transformation." In doing so, he would need to be able to describe the new software development and delivery process mechanics, the new teams and organizational units, and some of the roles key individuals play in the new agile paradigm. In addition, any such Big Picture should highlight the requirements practices of the enterprise agile model, because those artifacts uniquely carry the value stream to the customer.*

These words from Dean Leffingwell (2013), creator of the Scaled Agile Framework, presented more than six years ago, still echo in the industry. This is by far the most common pitfall of which many organizations struggle to extract themselves. Changing your software development life cycle from a linear waterfall approach to an iterative approach like Scrum will not have the impact on the overall product launch or time to market from a business perspective without first installing the core competencies necessary to create a culture that embraces ambiguity and a process of continuous discovery:

> *It is clear that meeting business priorities often require a quicker way to get things done. External customer transactions, internal decision-making, the very way IT operates to support new business ideas – it's all going faster, then faster still. Think of it as the business equivalent of breaking the space-time continuum: significantly increase your speed, and you can reach new, possibly more profitable realms ahead of competitors. (Johnson, July 2, 2013: 1)*

Follow this case example from our knowledge base.

Not long ago we worked with a telecommunications giant that had recently tied up with another wireless provider to launch a new product to the marketplace. Time was key with this product in order to take advantage of the competitive situation. To be successful we had to build new software product to support the needs of this joint communication platform and distribute to the customers in six months or less. Leaders from both companies looked at the several attributes of the project from a NTCP format, or novelty, technology, complexity, and pace. As the leadership team cracked the whip on the project team assembled for this new venture they determined that technology, while important, wasn't that new, and therefore not the focus of the leadership team. Complexity wasn't going to be terrible as the project appeared to be straight forward, but the novelty and pace were going to be blistering. Short cycle time and high ambiguity due to the novelty and pace screamed for the ability to begin building and allow for a schedule of progressive discovery regarding the requirements, led management to use agile for this release. All the software subcontractors were provided training and release framework, or to use their terminology a roadmap was drawn.

All of the aspects of software development were discussed and mapped to their respective suppliers, teams were created that included the business and quality people, and those that could be co-located were moved to new a new team work space in a central location. The team was set and the game plan published to ensure everyone was working from the same playbook. Team members met and got to know one another in a work space specifically designed with open areas to facilitate communication and collaboration, and private areas for reflection and retrospective. They learned their roles and were treated to special meetings with the vice president and program managers to ensure everyone shared the vision for the mission prior to launching the development cycle.

Software development and the associated engineering plans were well thought through and the teams trained in agile methods, but well into the initial couple of months the team realized that the business processes, those upon which the engineering process was dependent, had not been included in the agile life cycle. The procurement process, that upon which the delivery of hardware and infrastructure depended, remained largely linear. The legal process, testing process, data migration process, and deployment process were all still operating through fixed windows. With the peripheral processes working to support the agile methods from a waterfall cycle, even if the application development teams did three-week sprints, it did not produce any competitive business advantage. The agile project team however had not readily recognized the risk of failure. Their goal was to improve the development process, and a failure

> to make a significant difference in the business process management was not considered. The heights of irony were reached when the development team had a party to celebrate their completion of a high-velocity sprint while the business was struggling to line up all the downstream groups and vendors who were oblivious to the rapid development that was taking place.

The failure occurred when, as the development process did accelerate and enjoyed the celebration for their personal success, the company as a whole did not have the opportunity to share in the celebrations. In the end the business goals of increased efficiency and reduced life cycles were not reached, so although the development team's success was impressive the overall project fell short. In order to meet the prescribed launch date the rest of the departments that manage the business processes worked over time and weekends to meet the schedule, responding as they always did to fight the unscheduled fires. They continued in the role of hero rather than team member and as a result, there was no shift as a company, or even as a division, to the benefits of agility. Not understanding the business context and considering agile to be a SDLC initiative is a catastrophic cliff dive. It requires a wider definition of teams and a big picture definition of the process changes supported by leadership, quantitative goals and planned behavioral changes.

Implementing without a Goal

Implementing without a goal is another lurking failure. In this tight economy many corporations venture out to the transition without clear metrics or quantitative goals. Most CIOs are happy to see their teams transitioning to agile or implement lean. The "So what?" question is usually asked late in the process and never has a convincing answer. Always ask the "So what?" question before you begin your agile or lean initiative. Asking "So what?" is the only way to ensure that agile or lean, the process itself, is not the goal. Leaders never initiate an agile process or a lean process for the purpose of being agile or lean. Their purpose is to gain some sort of business advantage through reduced cost, reduced process time, improved quality as defined by the end customer, or for the purpose of eliminating unnecessary activity. Has the lean initiative trimmed the fat? How lean are we? Has agile improved my cycle time? Are we better off than when we were following a conventional linear approach? What is the return on investment (ROI) for all the training investment? Did the consulting dollars paid to the lean consulting firm pay off? Questions such as these really need to be built into the planning to ensure that, as the project takes hold and teams begin the work of transitioning the life cycle, there is a clear and expected test in place to determine success. This is accomplished by measuring the outcome with a baseline measure that supports the ability to answer the "So what?" question.

More and more organizations are venturing into this transformation journey without determining their current state baselines. To aggravate the situation further it is very easy to find a process consulting firm that are implementing agile and lean approaches with cookie-cutter models and frameworks, two definite red flags.

Consider this case example.

A large healthcare corporation implemented agile as one of their strategic objectives. Talented process change coaches were recruited to help with their transition, more than 10 teams were trained and staffed, and scrum masters were appointed. The agile coaches helped the teams to establish a roadmap for their sprint plans. Resources were transferred from their home-work location in order to facilitate face-to-face daily meetings and build strong team membership. New work locations were prepared to ensure they could be comfortably co-located at this firm's location. Every transition checklist item, if there is one like that, was checked. Team members from the business side of the company were recruited and gladly participated as the product owners. To make sure the business could support the added workload, they recruited additional support personal for their increased involvement. By all indications and as the feedback from team members were collected, the transition to agile was moving along nicely; however, after six months there was a leadership change and a new CIO took over IT. The new CIO, as is expected, was one day reviewing IT budgets and expenses and began to question the cost of the transition process. He saw that the transition budget had actually reached 30 percent of his IT budget. Red flags went off in his head and questions were raised; however, the teams had no good explanation and no reasonable answers.

Not understanding the target goal or ROI for the transition is a catastrophic cliff dive. It requires goal setting supported by strong leadership. Team members were not able to express the return on investment for the expensive transition plan. They were not able to express in dollars and cents how the transition to agile would impact their business plan, and therefore had no way of explaining the needed team membership and shift in project planning that goes with agile and lean methods in a way that made sense to the uninitiated business manager. In order to avoid change for the sake of change, or even the appearance of such, teams must be able to express the business reasons along with their project goals. The money needed to support the change to agile methods planned for the Scrum training and coaches was cut as the new leadership team took their places. Being able to express the impact on the organization in dollars and sense, the "*So what?*" of the change, is a necessary part of the mission and the vision for the future state of the company, and every bit as important as their specific project and unique roles.

Focusing on Individuals Not on Teams

As discussed earlier, there is a dire need to focus on the business context. Many organizations end up emphasizing their IT process changes to the exclusion of all else. Both agile and lean transitions run the risk of missing organizational objectives when the team members and leaders become myopic in their zeal to be truly agile. It is easy as an organization plunges into the agile transition to completely misinterpret the agile manifesto, and more specifically the first point of "Individuals and interactions over processes and tools." Even in lean, and this is also one of the primary reasons that leaders now shy away from Six Sigma all together, is the constant drive to encourage employees to complete different levels of certifications. Lean, as in Six Sigma, relies on a progressive training program of continuously detailed levels of training to support the use of more complex process improvement tools as practitioners become more experienced. When the focus becomes the process, or the training and attainment of the belt levels as reward for the work, there becomes a risk that the team may experience a serious lack of drive towards a common project goal:

> *Automotive assembly lines are common metaphors for the software development life cycle (SDLC); agility and velocity are paramount, so we strive to make the processes as streamlined and efficient as possible. Both processes begin with a proper framework and require skilled workers to build and unit-test subsystems that attach to the framework in a specific sequence as it moves down the line. Parts and subassemblies are made in huge batches and queued in storage depots until needed by subsequent processes. Eventually this collection of subsystems becomes a complete, shiny, new application/automobile that is system-tested and ultimately deployed to its customer base. Assembly lines are successful at building because the end product and the steps to produce it are rigorously defined and executed. However, having a rigorous process doesn't mean that assembly-line workers are mindless automatons working in isolation with no regard for product quality. In fact, in the 1990s, when the Lean revolution swept the automotive industry, many*

auto manufacturers adopted team-building approaches that mirror today's agile programming techniques. (Murphy, West, and Anderson, January 30, 2012)

Consider the following case example.

A product testing organization's Senior Vice President had a vision to reduce wasteful non-value adding activities in the department by 30 percent. Goals for the department and individual test groups were set, and the implementation toward achieving the use of lean methods was methodical including the development of organizational specific training modules and mentored project completion. All 700 members of this organization enjoyed rewards and recognition for reaching several lean goals. There were Yellow Belts, Green Belts, Black Belts and Master Black Belts in every team with more than 47 lean change projects completed in the first year alone. Each project was evaluated and chartered based on its own return on investment. The charter reviews followed a governance program to ensure the potential rewards were real and not inflated. The governance process itself was quite carefully reviewed.

Training classes were carefully scheduled based on expected employee participation in different geographical areas to prevent or at least minimize the disruption of work, and training participation was enthusiastic. Most of the classes were full, and managers actively requested more opportunity for their employees. At the end of the first year in the lean transition, the lean transition team met with their leadership sponsor to review their progress toward becoming a lean organization. They reviewed the projects with the executive team and to their surprise, when challenged with the "So what?" question, their actual outcome fell short of their targets.

The employees, it seems, were more interested in getting certified than implementing their leader's vision. When the leadership team began digging through the data to evaluate the list of projects and bouncing the measured outcomes against the target goals, the change fell way short of the desired shift in waste reduction. It wasn't that a lot of work didn't get done, or even that the projects were not lean worthy, but rather the projects that were accomplished were not the projects the executives wanted to complete. There were several difficult and controversial projects that were critical for the organization, but no one was willing to take on the hard, cross-organizational and cross-divisional work. Complex cross-functional improvements were lying around like orphans. Project selection, it would seem, was driven more by a measure of ease of completion and locus of control, and in some cases, as one may imagine, a decision of convenience. In the end, the project choice appeared to be driven primarily by how quickly the employee would be able to complete the project and gain certification rather than by project necessity and goal attainment.

The lesson learned for this organization was that agile and lean transitions do not just need senior management sponsorship; they need senior management attention and to be driven from the top. Governance of project selection and controls needs to be focused on the basics of quality assurance to ensure that the program that is defined is properly implemented and tracked. This means that a process of review based on prescribed project goals and process controls should be independently assessed for compliance to well-defined leadership expectations. If the goals are targeted towards individuals, teams, functions or departments it is likely that the outcomes will be driven by individual desires – a catastrophic cliff dive. Effective goal attainment requires holistic teams that are formed and driven by the top. Typical agile approaches are better prepared to handle this than lean teams. It is a huge shift for a typical lean methodology to consider directed teams for lean projects.

Focusing on Process Changes and Not on Customer Value Creation

Customer value creation and understanding value chains might sound to many like clichés from the MBA classroom of the 1980s. The concept of value chains as a decision support tool was added onto the competitive strategies paradigm developed by Michael Porter as early as 1979. In Porter's value chain model, Inbound Logistics, Operations, Outbound Logistics, Marketing and Sales and Service are categorized as primary activities. Secondary activities include Procurement, Human Resource management, Technological Development and Infrastructure (Porter and Millar, 1985; Porter, 2008). The appropriate level for constructing a value chain using this model is at the business unit, and not, as many would think, the division or perhaps even the corporate level. In a value chain model, the product is traced through activities of a chain in order, and at each activity the product gains some value. The chain of activities gives the products more added value than the sum of added values of all activities.

However, there is a huge resurgence of customer value modeling in the industry today. This is likely a part of the "small earth" phenomenon. CEOs are seeing competition heat up like a local gas station price war of the late 1970s in the USA. This time, however, participants in this price war may be separated by thousands of miles, and yet still be competing as though their store fronts face one another from across the street. Due to the level of competition, industry leaders are starting to focus on customer experience as a way of differentiating their products like they have never done before. According to Forrester (2010), over the past two years, consumer technology adoption and market forces have catapulted the field of customer experience into strategic stature. And as customer experience professionals work to change how their organizations operate, lean is adding both credibility and scale to customer experience improvement efforts. The reason for this minor digression is to layout the future of the landscape where customer experience and customer value are critical components of organizational priorities in the coming years.

Having determined the future of work and the role of customer value, it is a huge cliff dive if customer experience or customer value metrics are not integrated with your transformation efforts. Unlike the other pitfalls we have discussed, this one is not so easily recognized.

Consider this case example.

A major Customer Service organization worked on their agile and lean implementation for more than six months. The senior executives, including the CIO and group heads, were reviewing the successes of the lean transformation effort and were particularly excited by one of the presentations. The lean change was a project designed to reduce waste in the form of "noise" in the alerts the network team received every day. Alerts would come in to the team in the form of trouble calls and requests for assistance from employees with network problems such as access other interruptions to their daily work activities. The improvement received enthusiastic applause when it was noted that the alert volume was reduced by 50 percent with a project return of more than half a million US dollars based on this improvement.

Executives were so excited at having a project with high returns in waste reduction that the project was showcased as the improvement of the month and celebrations shared across media venues such as close caption television and mass emails to everyone in the division to tell of a great success in employee engagement and the use of lean methods. Employees were highly motivated by the success and the opportunity to share their work, but enthusiasm for the results began to change as more results were analyzed. As user complaints began to mount, the data was further reviewed to validate the outcomes, it seemed there were some important alerts that this automation effort suppressed. The delays caused by missing some very important alerts resulted in more expensive fixes.

This is a classic case where the goal of waste reduction was centered not on the customer value, but rather on the reduction of waste from the perspective of the process participant. The customer was not in focus. There are several stories like this, as we are sure each one of us could relate. As mentioned before, this pitfall is less obvious than the others and also most lethal. Management does not recognize this until these negative impacts snowball into a crisis. The impact of this pitfall is all too often an indictment of lean as a method rather than a failure to use lean methods correctly. When this crisis is wrongly attributed to lean and agile methods, the transformation efforts come to a screeching halt.

Pitfalls such as these are preventable, and can be detected before they happen. Subsequent chapters provide more insights on some of the proven remedies to correct and prevent such disasters. Using the same target organizations that we had used to perform our retrospections, we tried to probe further into this specific pitfall, and surely enough there are some commonalities. Following are the common causes that result in organizations making tactical process changes without working to improve customer value:

1.   not effectively defining customer value;

2.   not driving the change top down;

3.   not understanding all the levers that impact agility.

Not Effectively Defining Customer Value

Early in a project, as we pitched the progress of our division wide improvement efforts and the need to be focused on our customer's desires to the CIO of a major communications provider he held up his hand to stop the discourse. Obviously displeased with the direction of the presentation, and while emphasizing the importance of calculating customer value, the CIO suggested that we may be trying to over analyze the issue. He further admonished the team saying, both agile and lean are proven methods of which we just need to properly implement. He suggested that there are several implementation approaches from which we may choose, and "the smart people in the organization would figure out the rest." His suggestion implied that just because we hire smart people, that the implementation would figure out itself as though agile and lean were merely intuitive to "smart people." Obviously, with this approach, the agile and lean efforts struggled for the next three years. After several consulting firms and multiple leadership changes, he has currently established the directive to establish key customer metrics.

It might be worthwhile to delve deeper into the concept of value. In general, value of something is how much a product or service is worth to someone relative to other alternative things. There are several forms of value. There is intrinsic value, such as the actual metal value of a gold coin. If a gold coin is melted, and the gold sold as bullion, the coin, through the inherent value in the extracted mineral materials will remain beyond the removal of the workmanship. Another form is the market value defined as the value of which others are willing to pay. A third idea of value is a book value or legal value described as the legally defined value of the item. Finally there is substitution value, which may be described as the price of a substitute product or service. Ultimately, value in each of these descriptions is a cost proposition as perceived by the customer. We all want to maximize the perceived value that is the worth of our products and services. The simplest way to describe the value equation is the following: Value is the ratio of benefits divided by costs of generating those benefits. Numerator (Benefits) is the sum of the benefits and the denominator (Costs) is inclusive of IT costs.

The goal of transformation is typically to maximize benefits while keeping costs at a minimum. This is essentially the same as a return on investment model. Examples of benefits in your organizations can be spotted as satisfied customers, perfectly delivered applications that fit their workflows, high system availability and reliability, increased revenues, innovative solutions built upon effortless technology and competitive advantage. Examples of costs include direct expenses but also some soft losses such as the cost of failed projects, downtimes, frustrated users, cost of manual labor, rework and defects, and delayed releases. Typically, as a rule of thumb, innovation models focus on the numerator (benefits) and transformation models like agile and lean focus on the denominator.

There are generally two perspectives of value creation:

> Value Stream – A way to describe the addition of value to the product or service as a logical sequence of work flows through the process steps until the work is completed. Each worker adds value by performing his or her task and transfers the work in progress to the next worker in the stream.

> Value Chain – How a worker in the current step of workflow enables the worker in the next step to create value for its customer. At each step, the worker is the customer of the previous step. The goal of each worker in the chain is to enable the next worker to create value for its customer.

As we use agile and lean to transform the organization, lack of a clear value of transformation will prompt the implementers to focus on tactical ad hoc process changes. We can look at potential practices to calculate value in subsequent chapters. In this chapter, let us look at additional examples that would help underline the importance of this ugly pitfall.

Consider the following case example.

A software certification organization for a pharmaceutical company instituted agile testing and lean in their processes. The organization had over 700 people working as 17 different test teams, and managing the use of millions of test cases every month to validate the software product before it is deployed. During a recent review the test organization determined that there was significant manual testing. Without much debate among the test leaders, although it is likely all of them may agree, the use of millions of manual tests is considered waste and was immediately planned as a lean opportunity. Further analysis revealed, however, that only 40 percent of their test cases were manual cases and 60 percent were already automated. The management focused on the 40 percent and set an organizational goal to automate as much as possible. At the end of the year, they managed to automate and reduce the 40 percent manual test cases to just 19 percent. More than $800,000 were invested for this effort.

While it would appear to be a slam-dunk, the test leaders for this organization struggled to derive the return on investment for this improvement. Later it was found that the teams followed the path that most automation efforts will follow. They automated tests with the goal of increasing the automation percentage as opposed to doing the hard work to determine which test cases are most frequently used today and most likely to be frequently used in the future. Their automation hardly made a dent on the overall productivity. Retrospection also revealed that a productivity baseline was absent. If value, in this case organizational productivity, had been defined this investment would have been more meaningful.

Not Driving Change from the Top Down

This problem is so prevalent that many journals discuss it on a regular basis. The Business Process Trends website conducts interesting market surveys regarding business process changes, and a key component is the lack of top-down controls in project selection. We reviewed the impact of the process change efforts of one very large telecom organization looking specifically for the overall impact of their lean change effort and the effect it had, or not, on moving their chosen efficiency indicators. To their surprise, after more than six months of work interruptions and team member redirection to accomplish a long and expensive training and mentoring effort, the indicators had barely budged.

One of the first exercises undertaken in an effort to rectify the situation in their New Year planning was to review each project and check the alignment against the annual goal setting process. Planning for this organization is an annual event, and in the years past the process improvement project selection was always integrated with the annual self-assessment process; however, the project selection in this particular year was separated from the assessment analysis. For the year in question, the metrics used as indicators were selected and each department was requested to make the improvement project selection based on their department's own priority and interest. Department leaders were chosen and champions of the lean improvement with responsibility to guide and mentor the lean project selection and implementation.

As is normally the case for any volunteer effort, the volunteers were mostly volun-told. These folks were chosen because they are the *heavy-hitters*, or otherwise known as the *go-to* people when things have to get done. As good leaders do, they then selected some of their go-to people as the lean project leads. Now, by this time you can probably see where this scenario is leading. Very busy people choosing their very busy people, who then pull together a project team of very busy people who are asked to then take on more work.

Each of the teams chartered projects and worked them to completion, and by the way were highly successful in doing so. The problems, however, were problems targeted toward their own very specific needs and were designed around localized improvement efforts, and not the cross-organizational, indicator needle moving, projects that the top leaders had hoped would be chartered around organizational goals. They, by the nature of the workers own desire for self-preservation, targeted their personal project needs.

Not Understanding All the Levers That Impact Agility

Back in 2003, Boehm and Turner noted in *Balancing Agility and Discipline* (2003) that the risks when moving to an agile or lean format are genuine, and yet as the moved the conversation regarding the risks added that much of the perplexity is from genuine misunderstanding in the way in which agile and lean methods work. Some of that confusion is in the way in which leaders choose to talk about the methods as well as in the way in which the methods are implemented with less than enthusiasm. Lack of consistent definitions, overgeneralizations, and wrong claims of universality all contribute to the problems. Their conclusions, which are critical for our understanding, are:

- Neither agile nor plan-driven methods provide a silver bullet.

- Agile and plan-driven methods have home grounds where one clearly dominated the other.

- It is better to build your methods up than to tailor it down.

With that said, most successful lean and agile processes are custom built and organizations tailor based on their specific risk appetite. From a technology point-of-view, there are at least 12 levers that organizations can use to improve agility (see Figure 2.2).

PRIORITIZATION OF CUSTOMER REQUIREMENTS

Agile users want to develop software that is both high-quality and high-value, and the easiest way to develop high-value software is to implement the highest priority requirements first. This enables them to maximize stakeholder return on investment. There are several ways to prioritize the requirements in the backlog. Some of the most popular ones include the following.

MoSCoW

M   MUST have this.

S   SHOULD have this if at all possible.

C   COULD have this if it does not affect anything else.

W   WON'T have this time but would like in the future.

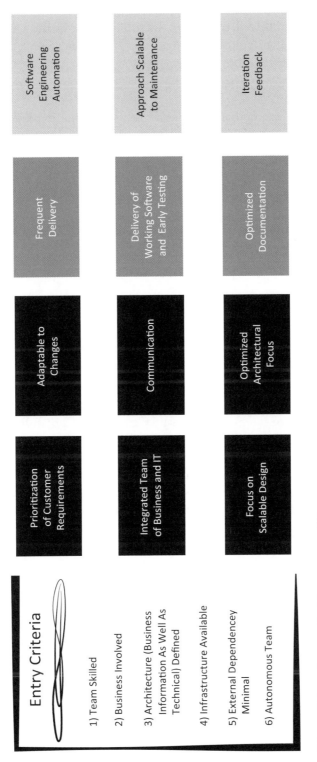

Entry Criteria

1) Team Skilled

2) Business Involved

3) Architecture (Business Information As Well As Technical) Defined

4) Infrastructure Available

5) External Dependencey Minimal

6) Autonomous Team

Prioritization of Customer Requirements	Adaptable to Changes	Frequent Delivery	Software Engineering Automation
Integrated Team of Business and IT	Communication	Delivery of Working Software and Early Testing	Approach Scalable to Maintenance
Focus on Scalable Design	Optimized Architectural Focus	Optimized Documentation	Iteration Feedback

Figure 2.2   Levers that improve agility

Each requirement will have the priority identified based on the acronym and is tagged MSCW. "M" being the highest and "W" being the lowest.

Business-value based

In this case, each requirement carries a business value it could potentially generate to the company. The business value would be decided either by the product owner or the product owner team. The requirement with highest business value is implemented during earlier releases.

Technology-risk based

In this method, requirements are prioritized based on the risk associated in implementing it. The risk is typically based on the technology. The requirement with highest technology risk is implemented during the earlier iterations.

Kano model

In this method, the requirements are prioritized based on the customer preferences.

Must-be Quality   These attributes are taken for granted when properly fulfilled, but can result in great dissatisfaction when not fulfilled. A very simple example of this would be the carton of milk that leaks. Customers are dissatisfied when they arrive home from the grocery trip to find packaging for their milk purchase dripped milk upon the back seat of their vehicle. Simply put, discovery of a clean seat will not, however, result in increased customer satisfaction. Customers have a basic and assumed expectation that the milk packaging will not leak, and it is unlikely that they are going to tell the company about them when asked about quality attributes.

One-dimensional Quality   These attributes result in satisfaction when fulfilled and dissatisfaction when not fulfilled. These are attributes that are spoken of and ones for which companies compete. An example of this would be a milk package that is said to have 10 percent more milk for the same price will result in customer satisfaction, but if it only contains 6 percent then the customer will feel misled and it will lead to dissatisfaction.

Attractive Quality   These attributes provide satisfaction when achieved fully, but do not cause dissatisfaction when not fulfilled. These are attributes that are not normally expected. For example, a thermometer on a package of milk showing the temperature of the milk. Since these types of attributes of quality unexpectedly delight customers, they are often unspoken.

Indifferent Quality   These attributes refer to aspects that are neither good nor bad, and they do not result in either customer satisfaction or customer dissatisfaction.

Reverse Quality   These attributes refer to a high degree of achievement resulting in dissatisfaction and to the fact that not all customers are alike. For example, some customers prefer high-tech products, while others prefer the basic model of a product and will be dissatisfied if a product has too many extra features.

Walking skeleton

In this method, the requirements are selected such that minimal, carefully selected, end-to-end features are built within a short span of time.

Validated learning

In this method, features are chosen based on the highest market risk, i.e. something that is not experimented yet. Release it to the market, get the feedback and apply the learning onto the new feature.

ADAPTABLE TO CHANGES

People think of adaptability in too few dimensions. According to Highsmith (2013), adaptability and agility are synonyms characterized by the ability to both create and respond to change. It is important to extend this definition to include both anticipated and unanticipated changes. If we know something is going to change – product prices for example – then we build appropriate flexibility into our software systems. Unanticipated changes, however, call for adaptation, a step beyond flexibility. The four dimensions of that adaptability are:

- People.

- Process.

- Product.

- Architecture.

Most often, organizations embrace agile development methods, thinking they will solve responsiveness problems, only to realize that an agile team and process won't overcome the complications of a 20-year-old legacy application with no automated tests, snarly, smelly code, and an antiquated architecture.

The core objective of product development in today's volatile business environment is to deliver a continuous flow of value to customers. We have to deliver a product today, and revise it tomorrow, and enhance it the next day, and augment it the day after that. Some of these changes will be anticipated in the product's vision map while others will be unanticipated, arising from unexpected uses of the product. Skimping on product adaptability (one quality dimension) has a significant impact on the future, and the future is tomorrow.

Of the four dimensions of adaptability people are the most important. Teams must move beyond prescriptive agile to adaptive agile, and in fact, move to the point where these descriptive adjectives of agile are no longer needed. Too many teams have a set of agile rules – do this, don't do that – which is necessary when learning agile, but lack the capability to tackle hard unanticipated changes on real product development efforts. While teams do retrospectives and reflections they often don't go far enough in challenging their own preconceived notions of agile.

An adaptive team understands that plans are hypotheses, that pivots may be necessary, that performance measures need to be focused on value and cycle time, that self-organizing teams produce necessary innovations, that cycle time depends on quality, that development is a process of learning new things and adjusting accordingly, and that change is the norm – not the exception. Adaptive team members realize that the most difficult problems are really paradoxes and that the solutions are temporary resolutions. They realize that change is the norm and not the exception.

Adaptive teams understand that process, even agile processes, are guidelines not standards. They aren't intimidated by what the agile experts say, because they adjust to fit their particular situation. Adaptive teams also need to explore processes beyond the agile basics, from Kanban to lean startup.

You might think that product and architecture should be combined in the list above; however, we separated them to give an extra emphasis to architecture. We worked with a product architect several years ago who built facilities into his company's product to handle multiple languages. He anticipated the need for this flexibility. Some in the agile community might say that this "anticipation" of change was the wrong strategy; however, building in the flexibility or capability to handle anticipated changes can save significant time and cost later. The secret is balancing anticipation and adaptation.

The Ability to Adapt

We also need the ability for architecture to respond to unexpected changes, thus the ability to adapt. Object-oriented design, SOA, reusability, re-configurability, specialized languages, and more point to the need to consider "adaptable" architecture issues early. Martin Fowler (2014), for example, has a series of blog posts on application architecture. Doing and being "agile" involves both developing skeleton architectures up front and then evolving them over time. Choices involving product architecture and the development environment will impact adaptability. Take, for example, the choices around mobile development platforms. Do you develop in multiple native languages that may provide a more sophisticated user experience, or in a multi-platform language that will be less expensive and time consuming to enhance over time? These are not decisions to be made halfway through a release.

A huge issue with the adaptability of products is technical debt. We were talking with an old friend, a long-time, not a friend of old age, and recently who had gone to work for a startup company that had been in existence a couple of years. In just those couple of years they had managed to inject an incredible amount of technical debt into the product and his strategies for recovery involved wrappings around old code, ramping up testing significantly, and judiciously investing in refactoring. His story, while one that may bring the geeks to tears, is not necessarily that rare. We once worked with a company whose electronic instrument software was so bad they invested nine months in testing and refactoring for what is often considered a standard maintenance release. There were no new features, and even though the product was being replaced in the not-too-distant future their investment in testing was essential due to the depth and breadth of their technical debt.

Technical debt is insidious because it sneaks up on people over time, and in the case above, sometimes not so much time. As technical debt rises, not only does development time and cost increase, but estimating becomes almost impossible. During the nine month release mentioned in the last paragraph, the team operated with only a very rough schedule. The product had gotten so convoluted that estimates of time to refactor and test were impossible. At first they envisioned a three-to-four-month project, but the snarly code took longer to unravel. However, management's primary goal for the project wasn't schedule, but putting the product back into reasonable shape, and, their customers were ecstatic about the new release because it didn't crash anymore!

Adaptability, the ability to respond to both anticipated and unanticipated changes, grows in importance as the rate of business and technology change accelerates. It's not enough to have agile people, or agile processes, or an adaptive architecture, or low technical debt – you need all four.

FREQUENT DELIVERY

So how frequent is frequent? Scrum says break things into 30-day sprints. That's certainly frequent compared to most traditional software development projects. Consider a major back-office system in a large corporation, with traditional projects running from six to 12-plus months, and all the implications of a big rollout and potentially training to hundreds of users. Thirty days might be a bit too frequent in that case. The overhead of releasing the software is just too large to be practical on such a regular basis. But consider a website, a web-based product, or even more dynamic something like a blog. There's no rollout overhead. It's an automated central deployment to all users, and for the blog it's a single click. No one is paying for the service. If something is wrong, no one dies, and it can be rolled back as quickly as it is deployed. There may be thousands of users, even millions of users of a website every month, but none of them need to be trained and you can evaluate the impact on the user experience, and the user's behavior, through metrics within 24 hours and on an ongoing basis. In that scenario, 30 days is a lifetime!

The Value of First-Mover Advantage

Competitors will not wait and speed-to-market is a significant competitive edge. The value of first-mover advantage is potentially enormous. Whilst it's not always the case, research shows that those first to market 80 percent of the time win; and end up clear market leaders. So how frequent is frequent enough? This is determined based on your organization, your product, your market and your customers. What is fairly important is to make this a positive decision to decide what's appropriate for you and then to stick, if you can, to a regular release cycle. A regular release cycle allows you to plan. It allows your infrastructure and operations teams to plan. It allows your business colleagues to plan, and because agile development works to a fixed timescale, these plans are assured. A regular release cycle also allows you to learn more effectively.

Your estimating might be good, it might be bad, but hopefully it's at least consistent. If you estimate features at a granular level, ideally less than one day, and track your velocity which is how much of your estimate you actually delivered in each sprint, in time you'll begin to understand your normal delivery rate. When you understand this well, you'll be surprised how predictable you can be. Let's face it, managing expectations is really all about predictability. If people know what to expect, they're generally happy, and if they don't, they're not so happy. They may even be furious, so with agile development focus on frequent delivery of products. Perhaps even more importantly, the focus is on consistent delivery of products.

There's not much to summarize here but to say it in two words, the third principle is about Frequency of Delivery.

SOFTWARE ENGINEERING AUTOMATION

Automation needs to be a holistic, end-to-end and all-inclusive endeavor. Typically, the following are obvious processes for automation:

Innovation management.

Product life cycle management.

Software code generators/Automated tools.

Automated Testing.

Automated configuration/Release management.

Deployment tools.

Based on an article in *The Economist*'s Intelligence Unit (2009), the market turbulence of recent years may foreshadow a new phase of globalization. In this new model of economic uncertainty, and one in which volatility remains high and is likely to remain a constant companion. In this time we have seen many ups and downs in the financial markets and major upheavals in national security, regulatory environments, and social stability. Even after the current recession lifts, underlying fluctuations in energy, commodity and currency rates, the emergence of new and non-traditional competitors, and rising customer demands will continue to roil traditional business and operating models for some time to come. To be competitive, companies may find themselves in a Houdini-like twist. Houdini, considered by many to be an artist of the heart-stopping, lock-removing and knot escapee, set the standard for the inexplicable survival in extreme uncertainty. How he did it is somewhat easy to explain when one considers his exemplary physical conditioning in agility and maximization of competencies in planning, risk management, and early preparation.

How can an organization respond quickly and nimbly to the changing environment without getting caught in the knots? In today's knowledge age, the ability to transform information into insight in response to market movements is a core competency every organization must have to ensure sustainability. Companies must consider new ways to make their processes more flexible. There are many challenges and rewards for organizational agility, particularly in tough economic times.

Organizational agility is a core differentiator in today's rapidly changing business environment. Nearly 90 percent of executives surveyed by *The Economist* Intelligence Unit believe that organizational agility is critical for business success. One-half of all chief executive officers (CEOs) and chief information officers (CIOs) polled agree that rapid decision-making and execution are not only important, but essential to a company's competitive standing. Agility may also be linked to profitable growth: research conducted at the Massachusetts Institute of Technology (MIT) suggests that agile firms grow revenue 37 percent faster and generate 30 percent higher profits than non-agile companies.

Yet most companies admit they are not flexible enough to compete successfully. While the overwhelming majority of executives view organizational agility as a competitive necessity, actual business readiness is mixed. More than one-quarter of respondents say that their organization is at a competitive disadvantage because it is not agile enough to anticipate fundamental marketplace shifts. Part of the difficulty in improving agility is the view that many Chief Executives (CEOs) have regarding agility. According to PWC (Global CEO Survey, 2013), many CEOs view agility not in terms of the methodology, but rather in their ability to quickly adjust direction and momentum rather than the flexibility and velocity with which the agile methodologist views true agility. Agility appears to be found in the nineties strategy of pushing the decision-making to the lowest reasonable level in the organization by drawing in more lower level managers into the strategic planning process. Nearly 80 percent of CEOs polled reported involving lower level managers in the planning process.

Internal barriers, often erected at the highest levels of the organization stall agile and lean change efforts. More than 80 percent of survey respondents in *The Economist* Intelligence Unit's survey have undertaken one or more change initiatives to improve agility over the past three years, yet 34 percent say they have failed to deliver the desired benefits. The main obstacles to improved business responsiveness are slow decision-making, conflicting departmental goals and priorities, risk-averse cultures and silo-based information. These problems can come from high in the organization according to Global CEO Survey (2013). In their 2013 survey nearly 70 percent of CEOs reported having strong reservations regarding changes to their supply out of fear they may severely impact their ability to react to supply disruption events. This may be a problem in their perception of lean or agile methods as the reliance upon continuous discovery and value stream mapping to eliminate non-value adding activities, if not properly facilitated by trained coaches, can readily create lower quality results. Leaders need to ensure their people are provided the proper tools and communication capabilities to ensure they have the insight into the process changes and methods being used as way of providing themselves the assurance that all will be well. By providing technological mediation of communications and information sharing, the improvements that are enabled also provide the ability to share these improvements for replication and greater impact to the overall capability of the company.

Technology, therefore, can play an important supporting role in enabling organizations to become more agile. Technology should function as a change agent in the use and adoption of knowledge-sharing processes that can move an organization from good to what is often described as the best in class, or what is better described as an industry leader. Most companies lag behind in the process of gathering together the stories of how the changes were made, what impact the change had on the organization, and the necessary information to track and then spread to other areas the good outcomes. Nearly everyone needs to make more progress in transforming their knowledge processes to fit the demands of the knowledge age. While 64 percent of respondents say they are largely satisfied with the business information available to support their primary job responsibilities, only 30 percent indicate that they have the needed information to conduct their duties effectively (*The Economist* Intelligence Unit, 2009). Because technology underpins nearly every business process today, it can help those in the workplace improve their use of critical data. CEOs and CFOs are often forced to guide their organizations with little or no real information regarding how the work gets done, and the real-time outcomes of their process capability. Many appear to report that they know they are flying blind, but don't have the means to effectively build that data reporting capability they seek, in order to create easier real-time access to information. For CIOs, who are charged with simplifying and standardizing complex, and in some cases competing, layers of technology, the primary focus needs to be on improving systems integration. As companies grow in size, the desire for more comprehensive integration of IT systems across the enterprise also increases. More than 60 percent of respondents with annual revenues in excess of $5 billion cite this as the number-one priority for their company's information technology departments, compared with 42 percent of companies with revenues of less than $500 million (*The Economist* Intelligence Unit, 2009).

Leaders can gain a lot of traction toward true agility as they begin to integrate their strategic planning processes between the business and information technology organizations. By providing an integrated planning session the information technology teams gain both insight into the future plans and business needs, but also gain in building strong and knowledgeable relationships and shared meaning behind such plans. They will then have the ability to begin working toward the requirement discovery process essential for agile methods to function effectively thus greatly reducing the risk to both leadership control and business priorities when using agile methods.

Ward and Peppard (2002) speak of the IT delivery process as a comprehensive program of analysis of the environment, building toward a set of business requirements, and ending with a well-planned delivery strategy that compliments the strengths of the organization, and strengthens the weaknesses. Embedded within every IT delivery process is a basic assumption regarding quality processes. As Kruchten (2007) explains in the editorial of Booch, "worldwide economies depend increasingly on software," therefore, the effective practice of the quality profession is essential to the effectiveness of every IT project, and essential to the health of all IT delivery programs (Ibid.: 3). "Software is the fuel on which modern business are run, governments rule, and societies become better connected," and as Kruchten continues to explain, "have helped cure the sick and have given voice to the speechless, mobility to the impaired, and opportunity to the less able" (Ibid.: 3). As modern dependence on IT practices continues to increase, the urgency for effective research in the arena of IT quality drives researchers forward.

Ward and Peppard (2002) discuss at length the need for management to define the information systems and information technology (IS/IT) strategy in relation to the overall business strategy in order that the IS/IT Strategy may create the means by which the business strategy may be realized. The process is best realized when the management team is able to reach consensus regarding the IS/IT systems, and the relative value that each system brings to the organization. Peskin and Hart (1996) discuss the need for agreement one step deeper, in that, the agreement must also be obtained regarding the quality of the system design, and how to apply quality within the system rather than delegating the process of quality to the development organization.

Collaboration and Process Management are Essential

As is likely clear to most leaders in this new century, collaboration in planning and process management is essential, and most essential in mission-critical activities. There are many time-tried as well as new methods and tools available for different collaborative processes such as strategic planning. One area of necessity in collaborative engineering in the IS/IT delivery process is that of requirement engineering management. Requirement engineering, often the first point of failure in any information technology project, when completed effectively, can potentially reduce project failures and project cancelations, and should be a first point of collaboration between IT and business leaders. Lack of user input, lack of clearly described requirement statements, and changes in requirements once the project is in motion are identified as key problem areas to address.

Carroll (1995) descries information as a vital asset, and due to identification as a vital asset, information and those systems that manage and deliver information should be managed with the same focus on quality as other key corporate assets. As IS/IT systems become ever more integrated into the fabric of the corporate environment, design and delivery of the IS/IT systems becomes ever more critical. Carroll suggests that as systems are designed to deliver corporate strategy, participatory methods of system design must be used to integrate the user's view, and the means in which the user will implement the system in daily activities, into the design and delivery process (1995). It is essential to view the IS/IT delivery process as a vital strategic business asset, not only in the areas of design and function, but also in what is necessary for the support and maintenance of the systems. The support provided for the IS/IT systems is very much a key to the success of the system as the quality of the final product delivery. As leaders get more comfortable with agile methods and the contribution that participatory planning methods may make, communication becomes ever more important.

In *Agile Software Development*, Alistair Cockburn, discussing communication from the perspective of Media Richness Theory, describes various modes of communication that people may choose to apply when working together (Ambler and Associates, February 28, 2014). Communication is considered to be rich, not in content, but rather in the ability of the communication media to deliver reproducible content in the give and take of the exchange. As a message is received by snail mail, the likelihood that the original message is received on the first delivery in such a way that the listener is able to reproduce the same meaning upon an asynchronous reading is low, or as shown in Figure 2.3, the richness is considered cold. Figure 2.3 below reflects the growth in rich communications as we move from written one-way communications in the form of a white paper or snail mail through to synchronous paired communications that use both verbal face-to-face conversations and visual reinforcement in the form of a whiteboard session on the far upper right of the chart. While many of us may consider the use of email to be a rich communication media due to the ability to include many forms of electronic graphics to enhance understanding, the level of warmth in the media is still relatively low.

Understanding that nearly every project or team has an element of virtuality in the way in which the work gets done, the leadership responsibility in facilitating effective communications is essential to the success of the project. Teams must be moved as far to the right as possible in the richness curve.

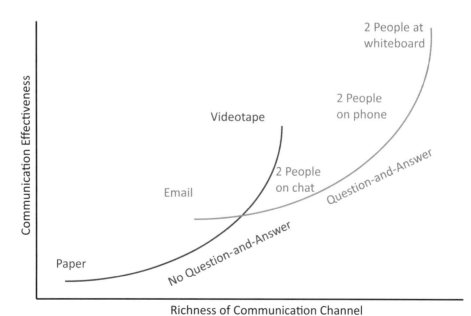

Figure 2.3   Communication options
Source: Adapted from Cockburn (2009).

Audiotape and videotape, when paired with an email conversation inches to the right of the curve, and when presented together intersect the question and answer curve, yet fall far short of rich communications. Phone conversations and video calls may approach face-to-face effectiveness and are essential when working in a virtual format as they provide a synchronous experience, and can simulate the paired experience of a whiteboard session, but still fall somewhat short of the warmth of a face-to-face shared whiteboard session. Moving up the curve as far as possible provides the rich warm experience necessary for complete shared meaning in the communication process.

Leaders need to strive to follow the most effective communication technique available, and yet remain flexible and scalable in the implementation based on the specific situation faced by their agile and lean process teams. If members of the team have the option to come together to work in the same room and produce a product based on shared meaning, perhaps it's best that they take this opportunity and yet share with the team in a video chat format such that the remaining team members are able to cognitively process the discussion. The output of the team may be a snapshot of the whiteboard enabling the team to capture and recall the conversation rather than to write them a document which will eventually be emailed as a hand-off to them. If you're working with someone at another location, then you'll want to set up regular video conference calls with them, have a shared information repository, and email regularly. Flying them in every so often so you can work face-to-face would be a great idea too.

Even with the increasingly virtual nature of most office work, the use of agile development processes have become increasingly popular over the last several years. These processes attempt to enable more flexible and adaptive software than traditional software development life cycles, but require a great deal of planning and facilitation to ensure communications are effective. Probably one of the main contributors to the success of agile methods is the dissatisfaction with the bureaucracy of traditional development methodologies in the level of detailed documentation required. Agile methods require less documentation for tasks and promote implementation based on informal collaborations between system stakeholders; however, the level of persistence in the communication does demand an understanding of strategies. Persistent communication, meaning the need to ensure that the shared understanding may last beyond the immediate conversation, does require the use of written communications in the right places.

Agile is effective in the development of requirements and specifications on an ongoing basis of discovery, and yet to ensure this information is widely shared and retrievable it will still need to exist in written format. Email and instant messaging are effective means of ensuring this information does persist and can be shared as noted earlier with those unable to attend the whiteboard session. While traditional software engineering methods emphasize careful planning and design, agile methods emphasize the actual software implementation.

However, this shift of emphasis is not without cost. Documentation is, among other things, used for knowledge-sharing and reduces knowledge loss when team members become unavailable, or perhaps simply move on in the project to a new phase of production and simply forget. Agile methods overcome documentation scarcity by significantly relying on constant collaboration between developers and users. One of the major time-wasters in agile project may be the time it often takes for a development team to re-orient themselves in the code when problems occur or changes in architecture or earlier decisions cause the project to be reassessed. Documentation can often be compromised for schedule when applying agile methods causing important knowledge to be lost or important communications to be delayed or missed during and after system development.

Relying on collaboration imposes a critical premise about the stakeholders involved. They must possess common knowledge and a common language to enable communication; however, in many cases, building these common grounds may be very difficult to achieve. In distributed development, where interaction is scarce and backgrounds are different, without documentation, agile methods do not suggest ways for establishing the necessary infrastructure supporting collaboration. It should be noted, however, that agile development methods do not preclude the use of documentation in their processes. Rather, in comparison with traditional software processes, agile development is merely less document-oriented.

Agile Isn't Anti-Documentation

Agile isn't anti-documentation. A more accurate way to say it would be agile doesn't do documentation for documentation's sake. Documentation gets treated like any other deliverable on an agile project. It gets estimated, sized, and prioritized like any other user story and then built into the production schedule and placed in the backlog where it is picked up by a technical writer or developer based on the need of the project production timeline. It can, however languish for attention as the more sexier pieces of work are chosen ahead of the technical writing. Where agile pushes back on documentation is as a means of communication. Agile practitioners prefers the warmth of face-to-face communication over relying on the written word and rightfully so where appropriate. As for planning document, it is a misnomer to consider agile to be an ad hoc, cowboy style, unplanned approach. Rather, there's actually a lot of planning that goes on into an agile project.

For the sake of argument, we have proposed a basic and fairly methodical approach to agile planning:

- daily planning with the 10-minute daily standups;

- bi-weekly planning with the iteration/sprint planning meetings;

- release planning where teams decide what to ship every three to four months.

But it wouldn't be fair to say agile is anti-planning. If anything it is anti-static planning, meaning agilists expect their plans to change and use tools like burn down charts to track and make these changes visible.

RETROSPECTIONS AND ITERATION FEEDBACK

Continuous Improvement and Short Feedback loops are critical for any agile process. Without a structured improvement process it will be difficult for teams to improve and without improvement the teams will perform worse than traditional methods. Retrospective, as a tool, is intended to ensure that problems, hindrance, headaches, and challenges are captured as part of the knowledge management and continuous improvement process to ensure the team is able to continue their growth in agility.

What is a Retrospective? It is a moment for the team to stop, breathe and take a break from the day-to-day grind. It's a chance to step back and reflect on the past iteration, to find things that worked well, things that need improvement and what the team has the energy to improve. Retrospectives are different from post mortems. Post mortems occur after the project is done (or even dead), when it's too late to improve that project.

Well-run retrospectives provide an opportunity for small improvements.

The Keys to a Well-Run Retrospective

In expressing the prime directive of the retrospective, Kerth notes that the team members and leaders alike need to acknowledge the discovery of problems and their impact on the project (2013). Participants need to develop an understanding and true belief that everyone comes to work to do their best with the skills and knowledge they are given. They must acknowledge that people worked to do their best with what they know at the time, and the skills and abilities they brought to the table along with the resources provided for the project. They did their best with the situation. The key here is to remind participants at the start of every retrospective. This is not a blame and shame: it's about understanding what happened in the course of the last iteration. The focus is on events and not the people.

Once you decide what you have the energy to tackle, set SMART Goals, or goals that, in the words of the management guru Peter Drucker, are stated using the characteristics of being Specific, Measurable, Attainable, Realistic/ Relevant, Timely. In the context of an Agile/Scrum team we would always make timely less than two weeks, so that you check back in the next retrospective:

- Timelines and Mad/Sad/Glad.

- SaMoLo (Same of; More of; Less of).

- Retrospective Wiki.

- Other potential agile levers.

Success, when making the transition to agile and lean teams, has many factors of varying degrees of effect. Some of these include a skilled team, the level of involvement with the business side, a well-defined architecture and the availability of infrastructure for testing, well-defined dependencies, and an autonomous team. Many of these factors are approached in later chapters of this book. The degree to which the architecture is clearly defined ahead of the agile development or lean change does have some impact on success, but will not be addressed beyond the need to keep your architecture friends close, and those who may not be bought into the change even closer. Preparation is key to avoiding the pitfalls in agile and lean transitions, and the degree to which you are willing to prepare your organization is the degree to which you will find success.

Chapter 3
Individual Behaviors That Enable

Agility and lean programs are less about the process of engineering and all about the relationships we build. Executives have long known this. The most successful executives understand they need to spend at least 70 percent of their time building strong relationships and only about 30 percent getting work done if they want to have a good and long-lasting impact on the way in which work gets done. Relationships, successful executives and sales people will tell you, are key to building strong teams and high levels of trust. The strong working relationships that are necessary to create agility and flexibility in the work team are built upon communication and trust. Building a culture where relationships between engineering teams and the business, along with a solid understanding of customer desires, creates a culture where agile and lean teams flourish. Relationships are the key to driving organizational results but to build a relationship we have to be able to connect with one another on a personal level.

Here is an example that most readers would have experienced at some points in their career:

A vice president we knew had a habit of stopping by the office of one of his managers to ask why he was there. Why was he in the office instead of out talking with people and getting to know them? He would ask why the manager wasn't at another office location or site talking with those people or perhaps talking with developers and asking them what they needed from the quality group as they began the task of leaning out processes and work practices. He would then turn and go back in his office and close the door. This was clearly a conflicting message and one that was immediately discarded as he turned his attention back to his work and forgot about the drive-by advice. Later in the week he would see the VP arrive around nine in the morning, say hello with a friendly smile and a swat to everyone's back before entering the office. The VP would put his head down and begin banging away at the keyboard with the door closed, a muted bridge call chattering away as he cut himself off from the outside world. After a few hours later he again flung open the door to rush about the office and suddenly stop at the manager's door, shove his head through the gap between the door and jamb and challenge the manager to get his name known, network, and build bridges as a way of finding those processes that most needed to be lean.

"You've got to get out," he would say.

"Sure," the manager would think to himself. "Getting on it," he'd think with a smile and nod as he frowned and turned back to his own work, door closed, keyboard clicking as the speaker phone droned in the background for another bridge call.

The end of his week was reserved for the Friday morning gathering of directors. This was our time to "read out" the week's events, talk with one another for cross-organizational coordination, and "come up to speed" with the vice president's doings. Meeting participants all arrived, lined up in their usual seat, plopped the laptop on the desk and got down to work. Heads down and keyboards clicking, the meeting would commence and one by one the directors would report their week, ignored by those around them. Some would watch, dismayed by the overt and rude disconnect between the meeting participants and their peers, until at some point someone realized they were all following the lead of their boss for he too was completely disconnected from the meeting.

This pattern went on for a long time until one day he was challenged regarding his own behaviors. The vice president one day decided he wanted to gather feedback for his own yearend review. He sent out a survey to his direct reports asking about his behaviors regarding communication, trust, and attentiveness to his directs, and the feedback he received changed the way in which he worked. The feedback was rough, but as he said later, necessary if the relationships were to be built that would create high performing lean work teams.

People accused him of not caring what they had to say and not hearing those things that were most important. He was "distracted, uninterested, and uninvolved" according to the survey respondents. He came to the next Friday staff meeting with a new appreciation for what the annual employee feedback survey had been screaming about for years; poor communication. Our vice president now believed he better understood the plight of his engineering teams and the annual cry for greater communication.

Our vice president entered the room early one Friday without his laptop and minus his smart phone normally found nestled in the palm of his hand at all times. As each person arrived and rested in their chair, laptop perched before them already in use, the meeting participants were personally challenged to close the lid and set it aside. Prior to the meeting the vice president had sent a notice to all meeting participants that electronics were no longer acceptable at these meetings. Not for himself and therefore not for anyone. We would, as he said it, give one another our full attention for he had now realized that his behaviors were the behaviors his own team was emulating. Contrary to the department's stated goals everyone had been watching his behavior and therefore determined that not listening was acceptable and expected.

Our goals had been set around building a strong cross-organizational team where all organizations functioned as one company and around one culture of openness and teamwork, and yet the behaviors he was displaying were contrary to those goals. After a few hurt feelings and a couple of panicked directors things began to change. Several of the meeting participants soon realized they were not communicating or listening throughout their day-to-day team interactions. When unable to provide a report without first addressing their laptops it became apparent to all that they were repeating their uninterested and distracted communication style everywhere they went. They didn't know what was going on because when their team told them they were not listening.

According to Adail (2013), only 31 percent of companies display a culture where the behaviors of the organization are aligned with the vision and mission of the organization. We should consider this report as an indicator of the critical new role of leaders that has emerged over the last decade. Leadership has shifted from the traditional role of command and control to one of facilitation and relationship building in order to establish the culture critical to teamwork capable of thriving across a virtual landscape. It is critical that organizations provide leaders capable of building a culture that promotes and supports the elements of effective agility and lean programs if the organization is to effectively compete in an agile world.

Choosing leaders capable of building a culture in line with the organizational goals is itself a critical new skill for most organizations. To use an old horseracing axiom, we must choose the right horse for the right race. Different types of competitions require horses with different skills, temperaments, and training or education. One would not take a world-class jumper to a barrel race or a barrel racer to the Kentucky Derby. A horse with strong focus and capable of shifting side to side to track the movement of cattle is not necessarily a great jumper. Even more important to remember is to not arrive at the Kentucky Derby if your goal is to win a world-class jumper contest. With this in mind, we approach the first of the Four Spheres Model of Agile and Lean Transformation and the need to ensure we are stylizing leadership in a way that pulls the team toward our goals.

Leaders Must Carefully Choose the Right Style

The right horse for the right race is an axiom meaning the leaders must carefully choose the right style for the right goals. Leadership style, personality, and goals must align with the desired culture of the organization. Steve Jobs built a culture of creativity and cutting edge technologies. Jack Welch created a culture that demanded quality and accountability. Bill Gates grew an empire around a culture of rapid delivery of new products that people want to use. While you may not agree with these leaders and their styles, it is a pretty well settled argument that their personality and leadership style were aligned with and for that matter drove the culture of the organization.

According to Bersin (2012), the CEO is not necessarily the key to long-term organizational effectiveness, but rather the leadership strategy, the culture it builds, and alignment with the business strategy. Selection begins with an assessment. We need to understand the requirements of the competition environment. Do we need the ability to focus on the steeple-jump in front of us or on the horizon? Is speed the key, or the ability to change direction at a moment's notice to stay ahead of the competition? By identifying the right questions to ask ourselves we can then begin to identify the right answers. Why is this important? Because we need to ask ourselves the right questions in order to clearly establish the goals regarding the culture of the organization.

The skills and focus of any two competitions are not entirely the same, and the same is true when choosing a leader. Over the past four years we have had the pleasure of working for three different vice presidents. Each of the three leaders had very different styles, but we suspect this is due to the need for very different outcomes. One was very transactional, one transformational, and one a mix of the two behaviors.

When first arriving to work in one of our past roles, the department was just getting off the ground having formed by consolidating several system test teams, and a group of people from what was once a joint venture company. The joint venture was bought out and brought in house as part of this new quality organization. This newly formed department of test engineers and managers came together in order to form an end-to-end test integration group with wholly owned responsibility to ensure all components provided by vendors and in-house engineering teams play nice together. This was a group of skilled engineers with a need to create new labs and new processes. They needed hardware and automation software, and they needed it fast. Building out new data labs and multimillion-dollar end-to-end systems required technical knowledge and project management. The group needed to act, and to act immediately. The group needed a plan that included technical requirements and design, and hardware, and architectural wire diagrams and power distribution plans, and on and on.

The leader tagged as "IT" to make this happen needed to be technical in training and experience, and transactional in the way in which he or she assigned responsibility and resources. Transactional leaders bring to the table a task oriented detailed agenda. These leaders are focused on the topics of rewards and punishment, schedule and performance, and often drive the team through direct supervision. They may have a tendency to ward micromanagement as a way of ensuring compliance with the schedule and completion of the task at hand. Defining activities and priorities, and getting it done was the key for the group when first formed, and transactional leadership was a way of driving toward the stated technical goals. When problems are not terribly complex or ambiguous and the goals are clearly defined transactional leadership is a good choice. The vision was limited and clearly defined; build new systems with the capability of supporting the current projects and build it as quickly and efficiently as possible.

People pulled together and got the work done. Equipment was specified, found, staged, racked, and configured within the desired time. Building out the lab was a roaring success. Organizational leaders from throughout the corporation came to join in the success and newspapers from the local towns and cities trumpeted the launch of the new test lab throughout the region. Work got done in short order and the consolidated test team got to work testing new projects immediately. With success came more projects, and soon the success began to turn sour as the test teams fell behind. Test directors became very hands on and lost the big picture view while their customers, both internal and external, began to lose faith.

A new vice president was assigned to turn things around. Upon arrival, the new VP introduced himself with a very simple and reasonable question; "What do we have going?" One would expect a quick hello and a list of project inflight followed with the backlog; however, no one was able to answer the question. The department went off on a data gather hunt for almost a full two weeks as each of the department representatives attempted to provide a list of their current and backlogged projects. So what happened over the first two years of successes that changed the landscape?

The department grew and the problems became more complex yet the management style had stagnated. The leadership style did not evolve as the problems and goals of the department evolved. The department was now operational and no longer developmental in its focus. The teams had real jobs and real deadlines to meet and were long past the engineering goals of connecting rails and dragging wires, racking and stacking servers, and lifting and landing leads. The employees were now attending meetings, building test plans, and executing tests and writing test reports and product evaluations. The team was now a team of knowledge workers and no longer functioning as hardware installers.

Please don't take the statement wrong. We all agree that hardware installers have the technology and engineering knowledge; however, test engineering outputs don't often include the physical disposition of hardware, but always include the technical analysis of outcomes, thus their participation is through their knowledge and not physical in nature, thus the term "knowledge worker."

The VP gave swift and simple directions upon arrival. The transactional piece – get me a list of our products – and the transformational piece – we need to be simple-adaptable-effective-customer focused, and agile – was relayed to everyone in the organization in order to begin setting the vision and mission of the organization. Each of the directors was admonished to define what these instructions meant to them and to ensure everyone in their department shared their vision.

Weekly meetings ensured that everyone was keeping up with their portfolio of projects and reporting on how their department was fulfilling the vision to simplify and adapt their processes and practices. New tools were provided to ensure the work was boiled down to simple "bite-size pieces" known as sprints to simplify planning and tracking. Measures were put in place and provided on a project and program basis using an online "dashboard" designed to give an agreed upon set of metrics that tracked progress toward project completion and attainment of the department vision.

Once again the customers gained faith, satisfaction increased and the organization began to grow. New projects were added to the portfolio and new employees were added to the roster. Soon, the organization became bloated as new employees were added each year in order to keep up with demand. As the roster grew so did the budget. Now this may seem like a simple problem, and one that many leaders would love to suffer. More money means more prestige in most cases; however, in a quality assurance or test organization more money often means more attention and more attention means more scrutiny. We began to receive bad press again and once again made way for a new vice president.

Quality assurance and test organizations are considered in most companies an overhead expense, and any overhead expense that grows rapidly is ripe for the chopping block. We had grown over the past couple of years from a small tight-knit team to a large multicultural group of more than 350 full-time employees and an additional 200 contracted persons.

LEAVING BREADCRUMBS

The new VP of Quality arrived from an international business consulting firm with a strong background in transformation and well-developed skills in transformational leadership. He was "leaving breadcrumbs" for the team, he would often say when asked about his leadership style. Talking and sharing what he is doing and why he is doing it is important so that everyone knows in what direction he is steering the boat. Upon arrival he casually invited each of the department directors to his office one by one and shared his vision for the organization. Leaning deep into his chair he smiled as he began the conversation saying, "We need to be flexible," in a calm tone and covered by a reassuring smile. "We need to know where the organization is. Can you do that?" he asked sounding a mild challenge as his face shifted slightly left and his eyes narrowed. "If you can, then you can stay," he offered as his voice dropped a notch to share the earnestness of the situation.

"Hmmm. Staying is good," was the slightly irritated and somewhat concerned thought.

As the manager left the office he said he would send a MS PowerPoint slide as guidance. The email was just one slide with a diagram showing a flexible organization and a description providing his vision and mission. The breadcrumbs had been laid. The group was to become a one-stop shop for integration testing with highly skilled, fungible resources, and a depth of knowledge to accept all the technological choices of their engineering counterparts, using the same best-in-class processes across the entirety of the organization. The vision had been shared and the mission established. We set about creating the project plan to measure the current state using a highly detailed and specifically targeted internal assessment that would lay a baseline to guide the organization.

Through the use of the internal assessment based on the behaviors and competencies needed to achieve the vision the organization was able to come to a shared vision of what the future state meant. Over the next six months the new VP would provide more single slide MSPowerPoint breadcrumbs to refine his vision for the organization, but no specific direction as to how to reach the end point. The organization directors were to work together to define the path and make choices that were best for the teams. Leadership was shared among the directors who then shared this leadership responsibility with their management teams to guide the organization.

Using this method of transformational leadership and shared leadership responsibility rather than the transactional style we needed early in the development process, the organization was nimble enough to make the necessary rapid shift. The teams started down the road to becoming lean in their processes and consistent in their practices. The employees learned how to improve from within the organization and developed the skills needed through both internal development and strategic partnerships that allowed them to rapidly develop missing skills.

As a learning organization it also began to develop a culture that was ready and eager to learn new skills and partner outside its own organization to develop engineering teams rather than the traditional, linear engineering assembly line. Together, the organization began to understand what it takes to accept ambiguity and shifts in priority or content and the ability to use data to find the right questions in order to accept the right answers. As a team, they discovered that they were ready to explore practices like lean and agile.

When an organization sets forth to build a culture around agility and lean processing it is critically important to make an assessment of the goals of the organization. Is it your desire to embrace ambiguity and explore the process of discovery? To keep running with the earlier analogy, are you are willing to share the decision-making with the horse as well as the rider? Can your management team accept the need to drop the old ways of planning in detail and let go of steps that are presented more as checks and balances and not truly adding value to the customer?

If you said yes, then you are likely looking to build a culture capable of supporting agile and lean methods. The next challenge may be consistency across the organizational roster. Building a culture that runs lean and agile requires the reinforcement of the proper behaviors. Everyone has heard about extinguishing bad behavior. We practice this as parents and managers all the time. Naughty children are sent to their rooms to think about what they did, and misbehaving students are sent to the principal's office and assigned demerits against their record. Likewise, underperforming employees are placed on a 90-day review to assess their performance in response to a prescribed improvement schedule. Extinguishing poor performance is a well-known and oft-practiced skill, yet reinforcing the behaviors we desire is a much more powerful tool when employed consistently.

The Danger of Inconsistency

Team members may experience inconsistencies as a lack of commitment or, worse yet, a lack of direction.

We once worked for a major financial corporation that employed both a chief information officer (CIO) and a chief technology officer (CTO). While the two of them had independent responsibilities they did share some resources. In this case the manager reported to both with a dotted line and a matrix structure with responsibility for systems quality across electronic financial systems, and with responsibility to influence the practices of several related quality organizations.

Their styles were very different, and in some cases incompatible. Our CIO came from the dot-com world and preferred the practices of Xtreme programming such as paired development and what we call today agile. Both of the development programs were very new at the time, and not well known or clearly documented. He did not believe in the need for detailed planning or a comprehensive program of quality assurance and testing, and was often at odds with the CTO. Our CIO's style was laid-back and friendly, unassuming and approachable, and yet intense in the belief that he hired good people, and good people will always do good work. This same style was the fad in the financial world, but the caveat the sentence always seemed to end with – if they don't do good work then they aren't good people and need to go find work elsewhere.

The chief technology officer was more a traditionalist. He relied heavily on his quality programs to monitor and control the entire engineering life cycle. Details such as requirement statements and design architectures were required for all of his projects and were reviewed and approved in the entirety to ensure everyone was on the same page. Project dependencies were identified and risks documented for every project and a suite of project and program metrics were maintained and reported on a regular basis. The CTO's projects were managed by project managers with their work assignments provided based on the priorities of the project. There were very few similarities between the two leaders.

Differences in their styles caused a great deal of confusion, frustration, and risk in the engineering life cycle. Much of the confusion came due to a lack of process documentation and inconsistent expectations among project participants.

> The CIO controlled the back office projects and infrastructure teams such as network administration, while the CTO controlled the product development programs. There were very few projects that did not cross over between the engineering teams. In the case of quality, this organization crossed over between both organizations for every job.

The effect of the differences in leaders was manifested in missed milestones, miscommunications, and in some cases extensive rework as one group would move forward to build what they believed to be the best design, while the other group would begin design work without input from the first. Project participants would often move along their own timeline completely unaware they were out of sync, missing important milestones due to a lack of communication. We do remember quite clearly a meeting of the combined project team on the eve of launch date when the network team announced that no one bothered to tell them they were supposed to order the hardware upon which the other team was completely dependent. Jaws dropped and faces blanched as everyone was stunned to learn there would be no hardware available for the launch. The team was forced to scavenge the production systems for underutilized hardware to confiscate in order to meet the project launch date.

It seems, when looking at the case and the way in which work got done, one of the key problems faced was the conflict in cultures between the two major groups within the organization. Everyone worked in the same building and yet the leaders created two distinct organizational cultures between which conflict was inevitable. With different styles and expectations the ability to work as a team was limited. Within the CIO's group electronically mediated communication was the key to participation. These teams stayed connected by talking with IM and email and held their meetings virtually in chat rooms, while the CTO's teams came together face-to-face in meeting rooms. They didn't have instant messaging on their computers and didn't have access to the technologies used by their project counterparts. Although we all worked within the same building, and we often saw one another on a regular basis we were separated by a virtual wall. The CTO teams were excluded from the CIO's *in* clique and unable to participate. The next of the Four Spheres Model of Agile and Lean Transformation is designed to ensure we meet the needs of the team and ensure the environment in which they work is designed to facilitate teamwork and reinforce the behaviors we strive to encourage.

Build an Environment For Teamwork

For team members separated by any of the elements of virtuality, building the ability to communicate effectively is essential to creating shared meaning around the vision and mission that establish and support the behaviors needed to compete effectively. Providing clarity around the direction of the organization is essential to developing an environment where team members may come together and share the responsibility for the success of the team. To build an organization capable to participate and thrive in an agile and lean world we need employees that know how to manage and managers that know how to lead. Management is the process by which scarce resources are allocated across competing priorities, and yet in an agile culture priority becomes somewhat blurred by the need to allow employees maximum freedom to make internal team decisions. As leaders we have essentially shifted management from something we do to our employees to a process by which things get done (McCrimmon, 2010).

Agile and lean methods work best in a culture that creates a semblance of servant leadership as the way in which work gets done. Employees need to be connected with their team in a way that creates a desire to serve the team to which they identify. They must feel a membership with the team that causes a desire to serve and lead when the need arises.

Leaders within the team, while still leading, focus on the needs of the team and the team's capability to meet the priorities and goals of the larger organization. It is the duty of leaders to provide truly transformational leadership providing the vision, mission, and motivation. Transformational leaders have the ability and foresight to provide the bright light on the horizon that will catch the employees' eye and lead them irresistibly in the direction he or she wishes the company to move. A company, if we remember our management 101 course, is no more and no less successful than the willingness of the employees to follow.

According to Stone, Russell, and Patterson, transformational and servant leaders are analogous in their people oriented leadership characteristics (2004). They care for the employees' needs as a whole person and provide them with the ability and desire to care about the things that the leaders desire. They provide what Fabiansson called a home feeling (2007). That is to say a place in which they feel safe and able to be real, be their true self, or a place in which they feel they can take a risk without the fear of retribution or ridicule. The feeling that one can truly act as a real person and know that the support is there if they fail allows the employee to step forward and take a risk, to take the lead and not feel the need to always be a follower. This ability to step forward when the need arises builds in the culture the ability for distributed leadership to take hold. Building a culture layered with distributed leaders and committed team members is essential to effectively deploying an organization that is both lean and agile.

What does this culture look like, you may ask? When an employee makes a suggestion their idea is critically pondered and not dismissed. No one chuckles regardless of the difficulty or preponderance of evidence to the contrary, but rather the employee may be invited into a discussion of the merit of their suggestion. When an employee steps up and offers their skills to solve a problem they are provided the time, space, resource, and guidance to build and implement a resolution. As a manager or leader we all realize that the solution and the problem both need to have a relevance within the scope of the direction of the company before any action is taken on the problem, but this is the purpose of the vision and mission clarity discussed earlier. It is the guiding light by which employees are empowered to take a leadership interest.

Distributed Leadership

Distributed leadership is an essential characteristic of a culture capable of building and sustaining agility, and one that is highly desirable in building a lean organizational ecosystem due to the essentially continuous shifting of team member roles. While common knowledge in team building tells us team members require unique and specific roles, role shifting is extremely common in virtual project teams. A recent study indicated that only about 12 percent of team members maintain the same unique role throughout the life of the project.

Leadership is not, therefore, so much a role as a way in which people within a process or project act or interact. In the three essential characteristic leadership forms of servant, transformation, and distributed leadership, each requires a great amount of trust among actors as well as transparency and consistency within the organization. Leadership may even be described as the interaction of dependency in which people find themselves. More so, it may be described as the reciprocation of dependency as a depth of essential knowledge moves from one team member to another due to the progression of the project.

Groups and Teams

Teams function differently than groups. They tend to be more effective than groups in situations rife with ambiguity, shifting priorities, and complex tasks. Teams mature differently than groups, and often tend to have higher degrees of trust and member identification. To highlight these differences we need to look at the way in which researchers discuss group and team maturity.

Unlike team development as we have come to understand it as related to member conflict, the American Society for Training and Development equates group development to that of human growth and maturity (2008). Groups form in their relation to their leader. The degree to which members are dependent upon the guidance and nurturing of the leader is the guidepost to understanding group maturity.

Remember when you first attended that club meeting your freshman year in high school, or perhaps your first class of the semester in college? You may remember entering a room filled with strangers, looking around hoping to find a familiar face or perhaps just one person that looked as though they knew what was supposed to happen next? Finding no one, you probably surrendered and sat in what seemed to be a safe seat and began a continuous scan of the room in hopes of discovering a potential leader and soon simply turned your attention to an intent evaluation of your desktop or began perusing the nearest periodical.

When a group first comes together for any purpose that group is entirely dependent upon the guidance and will of the leader. Just like a newborn baby the group is unable to care for itself, and thus the name for the phase description, infancy. As the group begins to understand why they are a group and what their purpose may be the group matures to the youth phase. Now that the group has a purpose the group finds itself to be capable of performing the duties as assigned, yet still requires detailed instruction and guidance. Group members will now act as they are requested to act upon a specific set of directions.

As maturity increases, members begin to develop some well-tuned skills and a yearning sets in for greater independence from their leader and the ability to make their own decisions. The group enters the stage of adolescence filled with a sudden awareness of their own maturity and capability and a need to branch out and explore their ability to perform as unique individuals. The acceptance of responsibility, however, is not yet part of the equation. Often, this may be evidenced by the degree to which the undercurrent of complaining and grumbling permeates the group. At the adolescent stage group members will often go rogue, making decisions that appear to be contrary to the best interest of the group.

Finally, the group will mature to the point of adulthood and the full effectiveness of a mature organization. Members know their role and are fully capable of carrying the responsibility for fulfillment of those duties. These are the groups that appear to be well organized, efficient, and working together toward a common goal, and in lock step fashion. The leader is, however, still in charge, making the decisions and assigning the work. There is still one leader and the leadership is often transactional in style.

Groups are good when the work is consistent and continuous, the work is broken down into explicit steps, the process is well defined, and the expected outcome is generally known. Groups tend to prefer the known state, therefore ambiguity and change are not the friends of group work. Change or deviation from the norm are often met with challenges and attempts to ostracize the offender therefore maintaining the status quo.

Teams, on the other hand, once fully formed and capable are much more able to react positively to the unknown, embrace ambiguity, and adjust as priorities change, and accept new challenges. This behavior, though, does come with time and maturity. Team maturity grows through the discovery and conflict inherent in building strong, healthy relationships.

Members communicate from the beginning as they discover one another, their roles and dependencies, skills and capabilities, and the need for one another. They learn about their charter and what excellence means to them and their specific responsibility to the other team members. They join together as they realize that completion of their charter is dependent upon their ability to support the team mission and the strengths and weaknesses of the team as a unit.

One might draw a key contrast between groups and teams in that group members tend to have unique and contained responsibilities while team members tend to have unique roles and dependent responsibilities. Team members are often dependent upon one another to complete their goals and responsibilities due to the nature and complexity of the work. While the roles and responsibilities are necessarily separate and unique for each team member, their work is more likely interrelated with that of other team members. The process is often less linear and outcomes are much more ambiguous with requirements often discovered through attainment of a previously indescribable resolution.

In other words, teams, due to the formation process driven by conflict resolution and relationship building described by Tuckman (1965) as the small group developmental sequence, learn to work together as they work their way through Tuckman's model of team maturity. Stages of forming, storming, norming and performing are measures of the team's ability to deal with conflict, build knowledge about one another's skills, roles, interdependencies, and develop a healthy level of trust. Building trust is one of the key elements of the Individual Behavior Sphere in the Four Spheres Model of Agile and Lean Transformation. It is built in time on a bedrock of personality and information and lays the ground work for empowering individuals.

What is Trust?

Trust[1] is essential in a world where project team members have often never met, and in some cases don't even know your name. When trust is lagging, or in the worst case absent, project priorities and goals are at serious risk due to missed communications or leadership opportunities. Recent research has shown that trust is more often a problem most evident in the project leadership role more so than for project followers. This little fact can have a far-reaching impact on virtual projects since this same research indicated that a large percentage of project team members change roles regularly.

Role shifting is so common that, in the study, the researcher discovered that only 12 percent of project participants reported maintaining the same role throughout the project. Virtual projects are very likely to employ a tactic called distributed leadership. This allows the leadership role to move throughout the project team as priorities shift, therefore keeping the role of leadership in the hands of the most capable subject-matter expert and maintaining a high degree of momentum. Distributed leadership is a wonderful tool when trust is high and communications flow openly and projects are transparent.

Leadership is not so much a role we are assigned, but rather about the way in which we act and interact. In a distributed leadership situation, leadership may be described as the interaction of dependency in which people find

---

1   Reprinted with permission from Gower Publishing.

themselves. It is a reciprocation of dependency, as the power of knowledge moves from one team member to another.

Trust, Communication, Project Transparency

What happens to a project that does not carry with it those three simple attribute; trust, open communication, and project transparency? Trust suffers greatly and the project risk increases as the shape of the team becomes rigid and dependent upon the leadership to maintain progress. In the days prior to the dawning of the virtual work setting, managers were able to maintain momentum simply by managing. Transactional leadership was enough. Roles were prescribed, tasks assigned, and goals attained for the most part due to the skill, effort and determination of the manager. Strong virtual teams form not in the shape of a hierarchical chart, but rather like a project swarm shaped by the technological needs and knowledge of the participants.

This reality places a unique stress upon managers that was not present in past decades. What is most troublesome is the idea that virtuality may exist apart from the idea of geographic separation or cultural differences. In other words, every project has a degree of virtuality inherent in the way we work, and not dependent upon the geography in which we reside. The effect of virtuality on trust becomes most evident due to the way we communicate. Team members don't just talk, they instant message, email, and text.

Three Bases of Trust

When talking about trust we need to account for the three main bases of trust being personality-based trust, institutional-based trust, and cognitive-based trust. While we all are aware that each team member brings to the work place a level of propensity to trust, and their personal intuitive model of what trust worthy means, how team leadership and organizational management affects the other two bases of trust is not always apparent. Institutional and cognitive trust are highly dependent upon the ability to discover information about one another.

Institutional-based trust is the degree to which employees feel they are fairly and equitably treated regarding organizational policy. Oddly enough, virtual team members are not much concerned with institutional equity based on this study. Perhaps this is largely due to the lack of information available working in the favor of management. When employees cannot find evidence of a lack of equity, it seems they become unconcerned with the fair application of policy and simply assume fairness in this regard. Virtual team members it seems rely heavily upon the cognitive-based trust.

Cognitive-based trust, however, does not fare so well in this situation. The ability to discover information and make a decision to trust, cognitive trust, is the key to establishing strong, healthy trust relationships between team members. Team members need the ability to find information that answers their unique questions or needs for data in order to form healthy trust based bonds with their team. Gaps in data will be filled either by speculation or worse by rumor.

Leaders, in the case of cognitive-based trust, suffer the most when it comes to forming a cognitive decision to trust. Managers in a virtual setting, and most of us are in a virtual setting, must ensure that information is available and projects are transparent to ensure formation of strong healthy trust relationships. Trust allows team members to step-up and take the leadership role when the need moves in their direction to keep the momentum rolling.

Building Trust?

It is a long settled tenet of teamwork that teams of all types require trust in order to move beyond the forming and norming stages of development. The stronger and more developed trust becomes the greater the potential for team members to identify with the team. As team members become connected with other team members, finding ways in which they share beliefs, expectations, and desires for the future, they begin to see themselves as valued by other members. Their confidence builds and their commitment to the team and to the company strengthens.

A team members' view or perception of what trust means develops early in life. In 1971, Rotter described the development of trust in our personality as the reinforcement of expectations. As we grow, we learn to trust in our expectation of those we know or perhaps even in the groups of people with whom we have experience or knowledge, and thus watch for reinforcement regarding their behavior. We learn to expect that our parents won't drop us and that the sun always rises in the morning. We expect that our siblings are going to hate us one moment and yet love us once again when the mood swings slowdown.

Expectations are built up as we gain more experience and reinforced through daily living.

Suspicions are validated as we learn what or whom we should trust and those that we should not. As our personality matures there becomes a set of hard and fast rules within our personality regarding the trustworthiness of others, entities, and situations. Dark alleys, for many of us that grew up watching crime dramas or perhaps have first-hand experiences they may not wish to recount, are not trustworthy situations. These are now settled situational guideposts that we live by when determining what is trustworthy and what may not be trusted.

The personality of our employee arrives fully baked, therefore team members and employers have very little influence over the area of personality-based trust and one's expectations of trustworthiness. As leaders and team members our understanding of trust needs to go much deeper than this. Managers, leaders, and team members alike must actively pursue and reinforce behaviors that build trust among the team. Behaviors that create the ability to choose to trust one another are dependent upon the ability to discover information regarding our teams and our institutional practices. Do we know one another?

Cognitive trust is based on our ability to understand our team members. People want to know with whom they are talking, not just their name, although that is a start. Each of us would like to truly get to know something about whom it is we are working with. What are their likes? What are their fears? What are their desires for work and for life?

If you aren't convinced simply take a quick look at social media. Athletes, politicians, Hollywood stars, authors, CEOs, marketing gurus, and on and on – the list extends as the rich and famous seek to extend their reach into the hearts of millions by opening a conversation. These media-savvy folk from all industries realize they must touch their fans on a personal basis by taking a risk and offering sound-bite size self-exposure to their life. These people shout out their fears and frustrations, joys and happy moments as they work the system to create what they hope is a reality to which their fans and potential fans may grasp upon as a personal link. Their fans reciprocate, joining with their own fear and joy creating a bond as the conversation meanders through time with one self-disclosing glimpse building upon another as a community of followers is created and carefully groomed.

A bounty of information is amassed that causes the fan to choose to trust in a person or in an idea as they build a bond, and yet, neither of the two have ever met or likely ever will. The process of self-disclosure that allows one to identify with and create a connection to another, when the information is freely shared, provides the details by which a decision may be made to trust. This same process is necessary on a team basis in order that team members may find and understand their teammates in a way that builds this same strong bond.

Cognitive-based trust is dependent upon the ability to gather information regarding people. As this information is gathered it is measured against our own values and experiences. Each is determined to be consistent with or in opposition to what each may consider to be the attributes and markers of what may be trusted. Our biases come into play whether or not we consciously recognize those biases or how they influence our decision on a subconscious level. Upon completion of our subconscious analysis of this information a decision is made as to the trustworthiness of a person, group, or situation.

Silence is the Enemy

Silence is the enemy of trust. Where silence exists, or otherwise gaps are found in the information stream, people will find a way to fill that gap. Speculation will rule the day when team members or employees find a gap in their information search. At times the thirst for information can be so strong that any rumor will do in filling the silence.

While looking at the early career of a young work analyst in the nuclear industry we realized that information was king in an engineering environment, and most assuredly in an environment as complex as a nuclear power station. The analysts here – we would make a game out of filling the information gap. They worked in a mechanical maintenance department work analysis group responsible for the assessment and analysis for the repair of pumps, air compressor, valves, and other reactor safety equipment. This goes was way back in the eighties before the days of the Internet and the scourge of email spam and phishing. Back then information was shared by word of mouth and with the absence of the present din of voices flooding the Internet people talked. In these times we were dependent upon our managers sharing information with us.

The manager would walk past each morning, and perhaps once in the afternoon to fill the analysts in on whatever was happening that day, that is, if we were lucky. For information that was less urgent the manager would route a packet of required reading. This packet would route through the department using a routing list and as each person on the list read the materials they would initial the routing list and then plop the packet on someone's in basket to be read as they found time. The process was fraught with wasted time as the packet would languish upon a desk sometimes for weeks before it was read. Eventually the information would make the rounds, reaching the last person stale and useless.

To fill the information dirge they would often simply make up something. Anything that sounded plausible was good. It was interesting and fun just to see who would come trotting down the aisle with an urgent rumor to shed a little light on an otherwise dark, dank and silent work world. Once again, taking a quick view of the media business is proof enough of the rumor mill's place in today's home and business world. Entire businesses thrive on rumor alone. Take a look at how the investment and political world thirsts for real information. Television shows exist and earn millions in revenue each year simply by filling the information void. Information regarding our favorite actors, television stars, and athletes fill the airwaves, Internet, and magazine stands. The very desire to keep information to oneself is the engine that drives the need to fill the information gap with speculation.

The key to building cognitive-based trust among employees and team members is to ensure the conversation begins and continues. Remember that where gaps in the information may be found people will always fill in the blanks. This same desire for information about our projects and team members drives the need for information regarding the way in which we believe the company or work place is treating us in comparison to everyone else. We all want to be treated fairly and in a way we might consider equitable to our co-workers.

Every decision a manager or leader makes in relation to the application of a policy or procedure for any situation is an expression of how the company views the value and contribution of an employee. This means that when an employee requests a half day off to visit the doctor or automobile mechanic, the answer provided by their manager will be measured both by how well it adheres to policy as well as how closely it matches the last several answers provided to co-workers in a similar situation. We know that every time we meet with the VP regarding a project or perhaps have weekly one-on-one meetings, the first thing we hear from a co-worker is to ask how the meeting went. They likely want to know that the meeting went the same as their meeting, for good or bad.

SHARING INFORMATION IS IMPORTANT FOR MANY REASONS

We develop a sense of identity with our co-workers, teammates, managers and leaders, as well as to the team through the connections we develop as we find commonality and shared beliefs and experiences. The sense of consistency and fulfilled expectations create in us an expectation for the future that provides a guide for the desired organizational behaviors. Important here is how closely the fulfilled expectations adhere to the expressed expectations of the organization. With consistency comes trust only when the consistently reinforced behaviors are in harmony with the organization's public declarations.

Of course WE should clarify that trust may be good or it may be bad. Employees and teammates may learn to trust that they cannot trust in the institution if egregious misalignments in the organizations expressly desired behaviors and reinforced behaviors occur. In one organization of which WE worked, goals were established to move to agile engineering methods. We brought in high-priced consultants, formed teams to realign our engineering practices and identify the agile behaviors and procedures and created a steering committee to guide the transition. In no time at all teams set forth in agile fashion in an attempt to comply with the new goals. Team members attempted to co-locate and follow what they believed to be the heart of the agile manifesto, and yet when we looked at the teams they did not fully represent the organization. The teams were composed of the development team members, but the business representatives, quality team members, operations and network engineers, and automation and tools developers were not on the team. Our new agile teams were composed of the same old team members and conspicuously absent were any new additions to the team that would reflect the newly expressed way of doing business.

The right thing for leaders to do in this situation would be to stop the work, reform the team as directed by the senior leaders, train the members on the new methods and team based practices of a truly agile team, and begin the work once again with agile coaches in place to guide the team according to the established goals. We did not do any of these, and thus reinforced the old ways and alienated those trusting in our publicly expressed desires. Trust took a big hit from which we are still trying to recover. A few of the disenfranchised quality personnel were so upset by this turn of events that they asked us to be sure to mention them in this chapter. The final element of the Individual Behavior Sphere of the Four Spheres Model of Agile and Lean is empowerment, which as we noted earlier is often an outcropping of the trusting relationships.

Empowerment

The term empowerment has been around a long time and has to some degree become cliché in the business world. Whenever we ask about empowerment and the degree to which an agile or lean team is empowered to make decisions and implement the changes needed to be truly agile or lean the immediate response is "absolutely." So what does it mean to be empowered? It means they have the vision and mission fully and concisely expressed and the freedom to move in that direction with purpose and resources in hand. How to get to that common, shared end goal is up to them.

Consistency of purpose and action is essential in building trust, and trust and consistency are every bit as essential in creating an environment that empowers team members to make decisions and act upon those decisions. We as managers and leaders need to provide that environment that will provide for success. Failure, to quote Mr. Gene Kranz of Apollo 13 fame, is often expressed as "not an option" in the business world. Employees must believe they are allowed, perhaps not a failure, but the ability to take reasonable risk and not be punished when that risk is realized. We often talk about having to allow an employee to fail if we want them to succeed, but failure is just not the right word.

We want employees to know that taking a risk, a knowledgeable, well-thought, and planned risk, is acceptable, and that at times risks become reality. Problems do occur in business, but if we want employees to be empowered we as managers must provide an environment in which empowerment is facilitated, mentored, and reinforced as a behavior.

Facilitation is the act of formulating a favorable environment for the behaviors and outcomes we desire as managers and leaders to take root and grow. Leadership, remember, is creating a direction and vision in which employees may find a path on which to build a community of purpose and grow the outcomes from a fruitful project. This path must be cut through the jungle and undergrowth that rises from the uncultivated yet fertile ground that leaders create when they hire well educated and enthusiastic employees.

Such a path is created by clearing away the undergrowth and weeds created by well-intended and hard-working managers as they establish rules, tasks and due dates, and boundaries and limits designed to keep an employee focused on the well warn road. Now don't get this wrong. Rules and limits are important; however, when the desire is to create empowerment that builds in agility and new lean processing, new paths must be followed. The leader's role is to remove as many weeds, vines, and brambles and burrs that drag change down and slow the process of establishing new ways of getting work done.

This is the hard work that creates empowerment and allows the employee the freedom to be creative and take the risk to lead in a new direction. Leaders must be out front talking with managers and helping them to understand the new vision and the reason they must allow for new paths. The leader must awaken other leaders to the noise in the jungle and help them to understand that the noise is necessary and not scary to prevent them from sending out scouts to shut down the changes.

Nothing will restrict and drag down employee empowerment faster than the roadblocks and challenges raised by senior stakeholders. The perfect example is the role WE recently played in a large telecom corporation as change agent and process improvement consultant. Our vice president challenged me and a couple of consultants to create new behaviors and new practices that would usher in the use of flexible and fungible resources and ways of getting work done. These are his words, not mine.

We set forth by defining the vision and objectives of this new program. Meetings were called and employees trained. Facilitators were assigned to small groups and work teams to help them in creating their personal vision for a new way of doing work and defining procedures and practices. Teams were established to create the procedures and train the trainers to spread the word. Metrics were designed, collected, analyzed, and reported to drive the change. Huge enthusiasm within the department created momentum in the process of change and employees exhausted themselves with their extra work, but in a good way. People felt good about the difference they were making, and then – boom!

Senior stakeholders, the group directors, began to get nervous and challenge the employees regarding their purpose and the value of the project outcomes. They challenged the decisions the team members made and belittled the contribution of their efforts. In at least one case a director began to threaten the improvement team facilitators with being fired if they continued to work with their people.

Why, you might ask? Were these directors not involved in the planning? Were they not informed, or better yet were they not involved in the process of ramping up the project? Did their own leaders not inform them of the desired vision and the new direction?

Yes they were, and yet the challenges came, and grew creating huge amounts of drag and frustration as the employees tried to keep momentum. The directors resisted in novel ways that prevented the casual observer from realizing their deceit. In public every director was able to repeat what they believed to be their vice president's wishes. They were able to repeat the goals of the improvement teams and even show their support for the projects by praising the team efforts. On the backside of their public support, behind closed doors, these same directors chided and challenged their employees. They demanded overtime work to replace the hours spent on the improvement projects and threatened their project facilitators with dismissal if they talked with these employees without first talking to the director. One director physically threatened a project mentor to keep him from talking with his employees.

The directors became controlling and divisive when the vice president failed to clearly establish his vision for the department and bring the leadership team onboard. This executive simply expected compliance by his leadership team and believed the project team would bring them along by their own charismatic ways and ability to convince the leaders of the wisdom to follow.

Executive leaders must ensure the path exists if they are going to truly build an environment that fosters empowerment and new ways of getting work done. Empowerment requires transparency as well as the communication of their vision. Transparency of purpose as well as work is essential to facilitating good and effective decision-making by the employees and their leaders.

They must be able to discover information about their project as well as about one another and project dependencies to facilitate good and effective decision-making. Leaders do not simply proclaim an employee's empowerment and send them forth to do good. We are sure most of us have watched the movies where a king or emperor calls their trusted aid and bestows upon them the power of the king's blessing. This person is then sent forward on a quest with that blessing in hand, written and sealed with the king's signet ring to ensure that everyone with whom the empowered person has contact understands clearly and without ambiguity the power bestowed upon them. This is the kind of empowerment and leadership we need to establish for our employees.

Simply proclaiming their empowerment with a pat on the back and hearty fare-thee-well is not enough. Power, or authority, can come in many different forms and leaders have a responsibility to ensure that power is bestowed along with the delegation of action. The subject-matter expert and the authority of one's own position within an organization carry with them specific authorities inherent in their situation. As do the situation of being the close confidant of the boss, but when the boss simply delegates authority to an employee to perform a task the leader has a responsibility to follow through and make this declaration in a way that informs the employee and stakeholders of the change.

Employees and stakeholders need to understand the degree of freedom they have in making decisions and the extent to which they are able to exercise authority in getting the work done. The best way in which WE have found to make this happen is to ensure that every project assignment is empowered through the use of a project charter. In this document the name of the empowered employees are stated along with the goals and objectives of the project. Timelines are identified and key stakeholders named along with their interest and role in the project. In this way the leader fully establishes the authorities of the employee and the responsibility of the stakeholders in supporting and enabling the work.

Teams of every king need an environment and a culture that enables them to succeed, and agile or lean projects are no different. Agile and lean project teams are simply teams with a specific charter that must be provided with the ability to build strong bonds of trust and make connections with one another that last beyond a specific project charter. The team must be empowered by both a vision and well defined mission and a clear path forward upon which to build success using the authority established for the team.

In conclusion, Individual Behavior is the anchor for agile and lean, and therefore where the model begins; with a solid core built upon the behaviors of the individual. It starts with leader, who is skilled in managing ambiguity and fostering teamwork. It gives the team their mass that when combined with a clearly directed vision, the acceleration that gives true force to the effort. Proper behaviors are what maintain the flight when adversity strikes like a golf iron, ripping the team out of the rough when a path correction is necessary, and gives long flight with a narrow path on a daily basis.

Chapter 4
Team Roles and Responsibility

Let us begin first with what we mean when we talk about agility and lean when it comes to working with a team. What we are really talking about is the ability to be flexible and responsive in the way in which we identify, define, and fulfill the expectations of our customers. This requires that the development organization must move beyond the traditional boundaries established by the way in which work gets done. Agility and lean require the organization to now focus on the elements of their productivity rather than on their process (Nee, 2013). As Nee explained, leaders must turn their attention to the employee. Leaders need to learn to facilitate rather than dictate, and to work collaboratively in a way that embraces change.

There was a time when management had concluded that the customer was always right. If they wanted something done the right answer was always to provide what the customer wanted in the way in which the customer wanted it the first time, and on their prescribed schedule. The customer, the story went, knows what they want and when they want it. That, however, is not always true in the virtual work environment. Virtuality has changed the game in that quite often what the customer wants is magic. This change began in the 1990s as the data revolution gained traction.

Work began to shift from the traditional industrial environment to a data-driven environment in which every machine was implanted with a microchip. People no longer operated machinery that was now controlled by a remote computer programed by a developer separated by both time and space. People were no longer able to describe exactly what they wanted because they had lost the ability to foresee the possibilities placed before them. It happened to one manager in the same way in which it happened to countless people across the vast world of intercontinental business.

Follow this case example from our knowledge base:

A computer programmer stopped in the office one afternoon to announce intentions to perform maintenance on the program we used to track, route, and approve technical documents. At this time the manager worked as the technical writing manager for a large and successful nuclear power station. The department was staffed with highly knowledgeable experts in all of the maintenance disciplines necessary to maintain a nuclear reactor and the support systems necessary to create a safe operating environment. They wrote and distributed the work procedures for the maintenance departments and tracked all of this work using a fairly simple computer program that was essential to our ability to get our work done.

The programmer arrived at the office, announced himself and introduced his purpose. "I'm here," he said, "to get your requirements."

They stared at him in disbelief, stunned, and dumbfounded by his request. "I didn't ask for changes," he was told. "Who told you to change it?" someone asked, just before throwing him out of the office and demanding, "I don't want it changed."

He returned each Monday for the next two weeks with the same request. "What do you want changed?" The problem, it was finally realized was that, while the manager liked what he had, he didn't have any idea regarding what he could get and finally asked the right question. "What can you give me?"

Realizing that we don't know the requirements because we couldn't understand the possibilities was the onset of agility. It was at this point of awareness in the software industry that developers began to work with their customers in a mode of discovery rather than declaration. As leaders learned how to work with the customer to help them in creating a new awareness and understanding the many possibilities in their future they learned to collaborate in ways that allowed both parties to discover the requirements.

Discovery, however, created new challenges in the engineering environment. The developer and manager sat down and began to communicate and learn together what the needs were, and how they related to his project. Through this process they discovered some of the weaknesses in the current system where there were built in workarounds, and how technology could fix these problems. Together they discovered the requirements for the upcoming changes. Agile methods take the process of discovery to the next level in allowing for a continuous process of discovery as new possibilities are created along the development lifecycle. As the needs of the customer are discovered a little at a time rework is reduced due to the ability of the customer to first discover what can be, and then allowing our customer to realize what should be. In the second sphere of the Four Spheres Model of Agile and Lean Transformation the first of the key elements is to ensure an environment that promotes and supports the process of continuous discovery.

Continuous Discovery

By allowing for a continuous stream of discovery in the process, leaders place greater stress upon the roles and capabilities of the team members and their personal engagement with collaborative practices and embracement of change. Groups of developers working independent from groups of business analysts, architects, systems engineers, quality experts, and operations simply are not able to add the level of change and flexibility necessary for the customer to discover their needs, thus the need for everyone to join in the fun and become a part of the agile party. The differences between being a group and being a team will be explored in more detail elsewhere in this book, so let this suffice to say that a team, unlike a group requires unique and independent roles and responsibilities well defined for each team member. Flexibility and embracing change requires the independent groups to come together and form specifically assigned teams for each customer product or perhaps for large projects for each application or even function.

Teams that work in this way require a high degree of independence to explore new ideas, to be free to plan their own work, and to make their own decisions. In this type of environment leaders must be willing to accept the risks involved in giving up their reliance upon transactional relationships. Leaders, in other words, need to be able to set the direction and provide the expected outcomes and goals, but allow the team to decide how to get to the end and attain the goals. Teams, therefore, need to have well developed and well informed decision-making skills.

Employee engagement must be very high for this to work. Roles traditionally considered to be less engaged and less informed must be brought into the fold as a team member and fully engaged in the process of discovery, exploration, decision-making. This statement begs for an answer to the question who, in this world of technological communication and the ever present flood of information could possibly be considered uninformed? Historically, the role of quality was considered by some technology workers to be filled by those who did not have the experience or knowledge to play any other role. The term tester, according to Weyuker, Ostrand, Brophy, and Prasad (2000), had grown to be considered an almost derogatory term in the technology world. Testers were considered to be outsiders, and in many cases this mindset still prevails in the technology industry.

Teaming is often the default in software development where agile is now a household word and an expectation for new computer science students, and yet even today, as we sit here typing, those in test roles are often excluded from full team membership. One of the responsibilities as a quality professional for any company today is to complete a process assessment designed to measure our process maturity and provide data by which we establish the goals for improvement in the coming year. The assessment normally looks at topics such as leadership, strategy, planning, execution, and training, among other topics, but for this year we chose to focus the entire assessment on agile readiness. It would be interesting, we decided this year, to look at how well we have established an environment by which agile and lean methods may flourish.

Gaining Insight to Employee Loyalties

A key finding this year was in the area of teaming and agility, and how well our quality team members have been integrated into their agile teams. We spent a great deal of time and money to co-locate and train all of the team members for several key projects. Lives and projects were disrupted to move people together. Entire building floors were cleared of the current residents to make room for open team environments and managers were retrained to ensure the level of freedom for planning and decision-making necessary to make this happen. Teams were provided new tools to aid their planning. Anything for which these teams asked was given them to ensure they were able to act effectively in their new agile roles.

Yet, this year when we ran our assessment and focused our attentions on how well we worked in an agile fashion most of our project teams scored extremely low. This was both disappointing and puzzling. To better understand what happened we changed the focus of the end of year assessment to a more inclusive model that would provide insight into our leadership strategies. We looked at our processes from a strategic perspective with focus on how goals are established and pushed down into the organization, how well we communicate and engage our employees in decision-making and problem solving, and we gather customer feedback, and how well we collaborate with those departments outside of our own, and we scored pretty well. What is interesting was the comments from our employees.

Their comments allude to a climate of fear left over from previous layoffs and a lack of communication across organizations as well the problem regarding a lack of inclusion when it comes to team planning sessions. Each of the key items mentioned is a likely problem that relates to feelings of membership with the rest of the team, or perhaps limits the team members' capacity to join as a member. A quick look at Maslow's Hierarchy of Needs will help clarify this dilemma.

Looking way back to 1948 we see that Maslow presented a graphical representation of what we call unsatisfied needs in a hierarchical pyramid. Maslow postulates that a person will not seek to attain the greater levels of personal satisfaction until such time as all lower level needs have been met. Needs such as the physiological and biological necessities of food, water, warmth, and hygiene are requirements that must be cared for prior to the focus on one's personal and family needs for safety. Upon attainment of these needs safety will become the highest priority until met upon which gives way to the need for such items as work and pay. Each successor need, whence met, becomes subservient to the next greater need and so on the story goes.

An employee will not, Maslow tells us, seek to attain a higher level of fulfillment until all previous levels are cared for and secured. Thus the reason for an employee that has recently survived the layoffs, still coping with their feelings of having been threatened with unemployment, or perhaps even still wary of future possibilities of unemployment is deterred from seeking greater fulfillment in personal autonomy such as found with agile teams. This employee is likely to be less inclined to take the risks necessary to branch out and explore.

On the same note, if an employee were to experience an event such as personal or family illness that threatens a lower tear need the person is likely inclined to seek to secure that need which may indeed impede them in their higher level explorations of personal satisfaction. Leaders need to be capable of supporting the employees and team members in ways that solidify the lower level needs freeing the team members to be able to explore the levels of Maslow's Hierarchy necessary for agile methods to flourish. When teams form a membership, that feeling of belonging is based on a relationship of trust and an expectation that looks toward a future working together as a unit.

Having membership in a team is a feeling of safety, a feeling of home based on trust that has developed as the team learns to understand one another. They learn to understand each person's capabilities and unique place on the team.

Team participants come together with a shared sense of activity and goals. The team has a shared mission, and a vision, and each member shares in the exploration and discovery as the project emerges and takes shape. It is the lack of unrest that helps new teams and new team members find their membership as they come together to work and learn. New team members are likely coming to the team from a traditional setting regarding the lifecycle by which the work gets done.

Leaders carry the greatest responsibility in creating an environment where memberships can take hold and flourish. They need to create an environment where team participants are safe and able to share information about themselves, and other members feel they can reciprocate without the threat of over-exposure. Over-exposure in this context is caused when the rules of engagement are not well known. Organizational leaders need to ensure policies and procedures are in place to protect workers as they take the risk to allow their teammates to discover who they are. While we realize it has been repeated a couple of times already, we can never stress enough how important it is for employees to be able to find one another and get to know who they really are.

As this shift takes place teams will draw members from what is normally considered an independent test and quality organization, and hopefully pull them into the team as they form this new relationship. Team members are asked to leave behind their paradigm regarding how work should get done, which greatly impacts test team members in regard to what quality means and how it should be accomplished. As leaders we need to have some basic understanding of what is happening in the organization on the "ground level." What we think is happening is often not what our people are experiencing.

How work gets done is often experienced differently dependent upon our "level" in the organization. Senior level managers and leaders are able and expected to establish the expectation of how work gets done. Leaders will normally look to our process engineers and perhaps charter a study of the process to ensure the process is lean, refined regarding measures and metrics, documented, and institutionalized through training. Work orders or procedures are often maintained in the quality management system or handbook and reinforced regarding process artifacts and audits. This process is more formalized in a regulated industry, and perhaps somewhat more lenient for other production or manufacturing environments. The key point from a leadership perspective is standardization and repeatability. We like to ensure the process moves along the lifecycle in the same way every time.

Or that is what we should have done. Often our processes are created over a long period of time through the process called tribal knowledge. Over the years people share information with one another as to the best way to get the work done. Team members bring new members into the fold by ensuring they are assimilated into the team culture. The process of assimilation will always include the secret methods used to accomplish a task in the best way. Managers and team leaders will always encourage the behavior because it makes the team more efficient – and oh, by the way, this does include the highly regulated industries.

There was a time when a team leader in a nuclear power environment responsible for building and maintaining the work instructions and procedures for how work is approved and completed. The process of writing these documents was highly proceduralized to ensure the right people and the right level in the organization reviewed and approved the procedures and work instructions prior to use. Representatives from operations, radiation protection, engineering, quality, line management for the specific work discipline, and the shift operations management team all were required to review and approve a procedure before it was deemed suitable to guide the work. The review process was a six layered masterpiece designed to protect the public, the work force, and the equipment by detailed documentation of a step by step work instruction that incorporated all of the regulatory, code of federal regulations, Occupational Safety and Health, and so on and so forth guidelines.

The review process was designed to be progressively less detailed as it moved through the review process with the highest level of scrutiny in the early stages of review. Process reviews took place at the end to sign off that the proper process of signing authority was managed effectively. From a management perspective, though, it made more sense to get the signatures of the available persons first, and schedule time to get the others on board later when available. It also made sense to have the writer sit down and talk through the changes with the signers to expedite the review rather than completing the review independently as was the procedure. A little fudging regarding complete independence was allowed to help the process along.

Problems arose when the people at the shop level discovered that the same person could fill multiple roles and therefore had signature authority in multiple places in the review process. This allowed in special circumstances that one person could sign off for many different reviewer disciplines. What this meant from a get the work done perspective was a complete short-circuiting of the review process, and at times only one person reviewed the work and signed for everyone.

How work gets done is often relative to our station in the organizational ecosystem. Leaders establish what should happen, managers establish what needs to happen, and workers find a way to get things done. As leaders we need to know what actually happens at the "get things done" level in order to ensure agility creates the flexibility and team environment we hope to engender. This means understanding the shop floor version of how work gets done as well as our expectations from the leaders. This translates to realizing that in the desire for expediency in the process, meetings may happen to review the agile backlog without the full team membership in order to "keep things moving" when all members are not available. Perhaps scrum meetings may skip the product owner due to availability or even to prevent disagreements in priorities. Testers are often not included if, as we noted earlier, they are frowned upon as not being full members of the team.

Membership, to quickly repeat myself, requires a high level of trust among all team members. It is trust that allows team members to express themselves openly, and it is open expression that provides the knowledge sharing and risk taking that makes agility and lean methods effective. Both methods require a high level of freedom and risk taking to allow members to ask the hard questions such as "Why?"

"WHY?" IS A SIMPLE THING TO ASK WHEN WE FEEL COMPLETELY SAFE AND PROTECTED

Just take a quick look at who asks this question most. It is our youngest, most inquisitive, and most vulnerable yet trusting members of the family that are always first to ask why. For that matter, our little ones, those that trust and accept us most for who we are, without judgment, and without fear will ask the "Why?" question and drill down to the point of distraction. They ask us why, challenging our sacred paradigms and assumptions because they feel safe and accepted and therefore free to ask. It is the child of this age that is able to stand tall and point when the emperor has no clothes. It is only when we grow older and wiser that we stop asking and we stop pointing. This happens somewhere around the age of 13 when we begin to believe we have the answers and begin to question our own safety and place within the family unit. Once the questions regarding their place in the family has begun, the hard questions stop and participation in the family unit becomes strained, the child withdraws and becomes less gruntled. This same process happens in the workplace.

Asking the hard questions is essential, and a large part of collaboration, the second element in the second sphere of the Four Spheres Model of Agile and Lean Transformation.

Collaboration Requires Risk

Collaboration is dependent upon the ability to ask the hard questions and to take notice when the emperor has left the safety of his chambers minus his grand suit. But why, many might ask are the hard questions needed? It is often the case during a complex project that many different strategies are employed by participating teams in order to come to the same goal. Teams may be dispersed across the globe, or working in the same office space, and yet the means by which they choose to accomplish their specific deliverables can be very different, and on the surface not appear as those they are in synch with the rest of project.

Sharing ideas, plans, and strategies, and having the freedom to challenge one another regarding the way in which they have chosen to get the work done allows all of the project participants to challenge their own paradigms. According to a study of students conducted in 1995, those that participate in a collaborative environment are able to perform at higher intellectual levels (Gokhale, 1995). They retain more information and are able to engage in critical thinking.

According to the Foundation for Critical Thinking, to employ critical thinking is to explore our biases and assumptions, our uninformed beliefs, to generate new purposes and new questions. Critical thinking requires a high level of trust and membership to enable these risk taking behaviors. Teams look different when they engage in critical thinking. I saw this most recently when working with a small team of quality experts.

Follow this case example from our knowledge base.

> The team had been working for weeks to identify and implement news ways of measuring productivity in our test organization. They met with testers and test managers from all areas of the organization and created the necessary automation tools to gather the data and present the analysis. Members had spent hours and hours of effort and time asking questions, searching out sources of information, presenting their analysis and making adjustments to be sure they

had the answers to the questions the test teams were asking. We had come together in the early morning in a small office, huddled close to the whiteboard because there wasn't really any space to do much more than huddle, and drew the conclusions for our own review. It was really some great work.

We had gone through the process of mapping out good business research practices and drilled down to ensure we had all the right research questions to answer the test management dilemma. In the end, when we had proudly white-boarded the entire discussion someone asked the hard question. "So what?"

"So what?"

"What's it all mean?"

"Why should anyone care?"

These questions deeply challenged all of the assumptions we had made when we formed our research plan, but could never have arisen except for a very high level of trust between all team members. Everyone trusted that the question was genuine and in good faith. The conversation stopped and everyone simply stared at the whiteboard hoping to find the answers in the data. "Good question," was the team response. "So what?" The next 10 days were spent in an attempt to determine the answer to the so what question. In the end, the metrics report became known as the "So what?" metrics.

Collaboration means we bring together varying strategies and methods, varying team paradigms, and differences in opinion to ask, analyze, evaluate, and answer the hard questions. Since agile and lean methods are inherently collaborative, meaning they likely won't function well without the ability to collaborate, then we need to truly understand how it affects our project teams. Collaboration at its simplest form is the act of working with someone else in the production of a product or service, thus it is the act of giving of one's skills and ability to the greater good of the success of the team.

This requires teams to have respect for their members and to provide them the opportunity and ability to participate. There are two team members in an agile or lean environment that often struggle to gain the ability to participate early in the project life cycle. Testers struggle to gain access to the developers plans early enough to make a difference, although, as many researchers will tell the story, they have a great deal of insight into the way in which the application or system behaves as opposed to how it is supposed to behave. Customers, as the second of the oft estranged team members, have the insight regarding how the application or system will be used as opposed to the business insight of the analyst regarding how they hope to use the product. With respect to their role, the customer and their unique relationship with the product are the very purpose for the use of agility.

For collaboration to be effective, and early in the process of forming the collaborative relationship rather than a year down the road, team members must have the clarity of purpose that comes with effective team building. Members on the collaboration team must know one another's roles and responsibilities and clearly understand the mission and vision. I realize that this has likely become a key theme and perhaps, to use another American euphemism, beaten this horse to a great extent, but the theme must carry on. Clarity of purpose is the first key and essential element for every team member in order to ensure effective collaboration of every member. Let's focus on only one role to make this point.

The tester on the project is historically described as an outsider in the project team. Their role was often defined as necessarily independent from the development and architectural team members in order to ensure their work was uninhibited by relationships and capable to taking a clear third party view of the project. With the move to agile teams, the testers now must take a membership place on the project team and work in collaboration rather than independently. To provide the clarity for their collaboration, they bring to the table the ability to define the full playing field for the development team. As an example, this means they can describe the clarity and probability in the requirement discussion regarding the testability and validation of requirements, and planning for reliability and performance, as well as the probability of occurrence regarding obscure scenarios in the testing of logic. Everyone has a place on the team and a specific and unique role to play in the collaboration process.

As the collaboration planning is advanced, the team should look to the customer to express the way in which they intend to use the application or system. How the product is to be used is often very different from the business requirements as expressed by the business analyst on the team. Take for example earlier discussion regarding the technical writing team. The software in question was designed by the business analyst to provide for the cataloging of technical procedures for use in the maintenance and operations of the nuclear power station. It managed the approval and distribution process and therefore captured the date of publication and the required distribution points for each of the documents as it is placed in service. What it didn't do is meet the needs of the end user. In practice, the user of the software was trying to manage the workflow of the process in order to expedite the review process in order to keep the current document in the field for use by the maintenance and operations teams to ensure they were working to the latest revision of regulatory requirements. We needed a system that not only tracked the distribution process, but also the review process so we could find the latest revision and ensure it made it to the field before the next use of the procedure. Only the customer could have known how the program was to be used.

A truly collaborative agile team will take into account what each team member has to offer the product team and be sure to identify these unique perspectives to ensure each team member has a place at the table. This place will be clearly marked and their contribution identified to ensure their voice is heard in the discussion. Simply having a place is not enough. The closest analogy to collaboration is the bench marking process. In an effective benchmarking process the leaders will first identify the current state of the process with a clearly annotated flow chart to identify the value stream or process flow along with hand-offs, measures, and deliverables. In this way the team knows what they are currently doing. This process holds true to build a truly collaborative team. The team will identify their team and the unique place each team members holds in the creation of their deliverable.

Once the current state is known, the benchmarking team will identify their desired state and the gaps as they are known today. Benchmarking then moves to the identification of what a partner, or collaborator may contribute to filling the gaps between their current state and their desired state. With this in mind, there may be multiple benchmarking collaborators in the benchmarking process, each with a unique offering to fill a unique need. This too is the process of having all of the needed collaborators in the room on a product team. Using this model provides the collaborator a clearly annotated place at the table, and establishes their contribution to the team in a way that offers them a voice in the team. By using this simple method the lesser recognized roles such as the tester and the customer are provided an equal voice to those team members who, by the authority provided inherently in their role, have strong voice in the development process.

Include the Right People

Another key element in collaboration is to ensure that the right people are included in the team. Ask yourself if they have a true appreciation for and affiliation with the team's goals, or if a person is simply on the team to fill a seat? This can often be a stumbling block to a lean or agile team as they seek to fulfill the requirements of a process method without consideration for the goals of the project. Business team members on an agile or lean team are often mistaken for end users or customers. Problems can be avoided, or created depending on how this role is filled. The end user is often and internal customer of the product, but are they really the end customer and are they plugged in to the goals of the project to participate in a meaningful way? Finding this person with the end customer quality perspective is essential to ensuring their contribution to the team is aligned with the goals of the project.

Winer (1994) discussed the difference between cooperation as a short-term and informal process and that of collaboration which is described as a longer-term goal oriented relationship. In this way the writer notes the need for the form of the relationship to be a reflection of the goals, reach, and intensity of the relationships. This means that if the team is large, geographically dispersed, and highly complex, then the means by which collaboration must be as equally far reaching and capable of filling the needs of such as team by using technologically mediated means of communication to ensure that all members of the collaboration have an equally loud voice in the process.

To summarize, the team roles and responsibilities form the wrapper within which the core behaviors are able to form a cloak of kinship and give shape to a team. Clearly defined and unique roles provide individuals the ability to understand how they fit into the vision and mission, how their skills, their energy, their strengths and weaknesses connect with one another. By continuously discovering the skill alignment, understanding the employee loyalties and fostering an environment of collaboration, this foundational sphere dramatically improves the Agile/Lean transformation success.

Chapter 5

Management Governance: Process in Support of Agile and Lean Readiness[1]

Governance and process are often seen as overhead when discussing the ability to support and thrive in an agile environment. Can a team that is flexible and performing at a high level of creativity and maximum freedom be governed by bureaucracy? Aren't process and agility counter in both goals and purpose? It only seems natural that agility does not require a high level of process. Isn't it? When working with agile teams we are confident in believing every manager has encountered these questions, or perhaps has even vocalized these same sentiments. The reality of the situation is, governance and process are essential elements in preparing for agility.

To be truly agile requires the ability to move ahead without concern with process and governance. For this to be successful, it requires that the team know and understand the constraints within which they are expected to perform. Knowing the constraints, while perhaps this concept is not fully intuitive, expands the ability of team members to make their own decisions and choose their own direction. When the work becomes virtual, as is almost every program or project these days, the need for identifying the constraints increases. Constraints are otherwise known as the governance and empowerment of the employee, and include the need for effective and timely training and human resource policies. The organizational constraints are essential to the development of both trust and freedom within the work place.

Providing the constraints, or otherwise known as the process and governance, around the work and relationships in an agile environment helps everyone to know what to expect and how to act. We have often seen teams that

---

1   Portions of this chapter are reproduced from *Trust in Virtual Teams*, written by Thomas P. Wise and published in 2013 by Gower Publishing.

attempt to become agile in their methods only to flail or even fail, falling behind and experiencing greater levels of rework. This is even more likely to happen in a large and complex project, and almost guaranteed when project integration with multiple dependent projects. Not a good prospect when considering that most corporate project teams can assume their work will integrate somewhere with another agile team.

Teams, like individuals, never arrive at work with the intention of falling behind on deliverables or causing the team to have to redo work they have already completed, but as with individuals thy are destined to this outcome without first addressing the planning. As my eldest son's wrestling coach would tell them at every practice as the adolescent boys would moan and groan through another round of drills, "first prepare or prepare to fail." What he was trying to tell them is that the time they spend planning and practicing is time spent in preventing failure, and not wasted effort.

Their wrestling drills equate in our world of corporate projects to standards, procedures, and training. When working in a software development life cycle, this may include coding standards. Practice for the wrestlers included strength and flexibility exercises that were repeated on a daily basis for every team member no matter their weight class or role on the team. It also included standardized and choreographed moves that must be committed to both mental and muscle memory to ensure that when a wrestler stepped onto the wrestling mat, that all needed skills were immediately recalled when needed, and did not cause the wrestler the need to stop and think. The wrestler, like the project team member, was able to expand their abilities by stringing together preplanned and practiced moves into an effective war chest of skills by having in their immediate employ all of the methods and yet well-defined limits. The wrestlers were not allowed to go rogue and think of new and creative ways to wrestle, but stuck to the constraints defined by the coach, and yet within those constraints were free to move, act, and react as needed to be successful.

Providing the governance processes and the standards within which the team is expected to operate provides greater development in the area of both institutional and cognitive trust and project expedience. Institutional trust, as has been noted in previous chapters, is heavily dependent upon the expectation of equity among all team members and project teams, and cognitive trust is the choice we make to trust one another. These same constraints that some see as limiting are the very constraints that allow for equity within the organization, and those that provide confidence among team members that leaders may perform effectively.

Follow this case example from our knowledge base.

In a recent agile and lean implementation with which we were recently involved, our peers and we held the responsibility to effectively implement the strategies. Over the past couple of years we had worked together moving the organization forward with a maturity improvement process based on a home grown program that was loosely modeled after the Carnegie Mellon Software Engineering Institute Capability Maturity Model, or CMMi. Each year we refined the annual internal assessment, with small tweaks, to bring our own model along in refinement to better match those such as CMMi, and each year we provided a measurement based on the assessment, and built out a year-long strategy of process change and metrics based continuous improvement. Over the few years by which we used the program of assessing, strategy planning, project development and tracking, measuring the outcome, and re-assessing, our process maturity did move what may be comparable to CMMi level one to level two plus a half point.

As we began to plan our annual assessment just a little more than a year ago we began to notice a growing wave of enthusiasm toward using agile methods, and around the same time became deeply involved in developing a lean process strategy for the division. With agile teams, or project groups that claimed to be agile, clamoring for attention all around us, we stopped our planning and hunkered down to re-strategize our yearend assessment. The assessment, we decided, needs to reflect our capability to support our customers and our project peers in the methods, and as was always our goal, to move the organization in a steadily increasing measure of maturity in process that reflect our organizational strategy. If our strategy had shifted toward agility and flexibility we needed to reflect that in our maturity model as a key element in the Management Governance sphere of the Four Spheres Model of Agile and Lean Transformation.

Shifting from Process Compliance to Process Behaviors

Transformation in any organization can be difficult and time consuming, at times tacking on years to what was intended to be a quick move toward agile methods and lean processes. It is at times painful and confusing to determine the best route to make the transformation; however, with a few guidelines leaders can choose the right methods to get the organization moving in the desired direction. Transformation can be prohibitively expensive when the traditional big-bang methods are employed.

The window of opportunity is often too small and the horizon too far away for the process teams to make a significant contribution (see Figure 5.2).

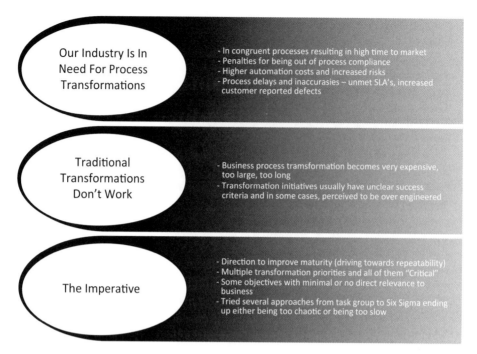

Figure 5.1   The need for process transformation

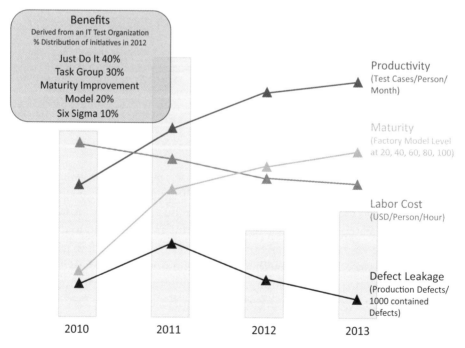

Figure 5.2   Benefits of an agile transformation

With agile and lean methods, the focus shifts from process compliance, while still very important, to process behaviors. In order to complete your self-assessment, the key is to determine the behaviors that your leadership desires within their agile and lean organization. To make this work easier, when working with our organization we chose to address the question from key bucket lists. In order to ensure we were able to address the difference between ready behaviors that a team may exhibit when working on a traditional waterfall or iterative project, and those ready behaviors born through agile or lean experience, we began our data collection with the type of project characteristics with which the respondent is currently working. The other areas of interest we decided to address are questions regarding the agile framework, enterprise processes, team behaviors, training exposure, and tools and automation of agile teams. In the same way we began our evaluation of the lean method readiness from a categorical perspective. In this case we chose the categories of process, metrics, training, and tools and automation. Although metrics was not a major category of our original assessment, we think that when redoing this survey we would definitely include metrics in the agile assessment. Agile metrics has become a major area of concern as the agile teams begin to expand and gain traction within the organization.

Each category was evaluated for the desired behaviors, and a list of these new behaviors was compiled under each of the lean and agile categories for our assessment. For the agile readiness assessment the list of behaviors or characteristics was as follows:

Project Characteristics

New development or release
Co-located
Team size less than 20
Project impacts few production systems
Stability of high level requirements
Product Architecture
Availability of test environment

Agile Framework

Availability of defined release plan
Availability of release cycles
Incremental releases
Iterative

Roles and responsibilities
Scope determination to fit release date
Process

Agile introduced

Availability of a defined agile life cycle
Transparency of process
Agile readiness of goals and targets
Agile readiness of project governance
Agile readiness of project reporting
Agile readiness of test processes
Agile readiness of tools for time recording, defect tracking, etc.
Agile readiness of contracting and onboarding

Process

Cross-team interaction
Test team's involvement during planning
Test team's involvement during requirement phase
Test team's empowerment for planning
Involvement of requirements owner for clarification
Involvement of requirements owner for prioritization

Training

Training on agile
Availability of scrum master
Skill of teams
Skill of test teams

Tools

Automated unit tests
Automated acceptance tests
Availability of test management tool
Availability of process for test automation
Knowledge management system

Once the list of behavioral categories was added to the categorical listings, specific questions that are relevant to the organization in how each of the categories functions were developed. The behavioral categories were also developed for the lean readiness assessment as follows:

Process

Current engineering/SDLC life cycle documentation
Engineering life cycle transparency to the test team
Roles and responsibilities of the entire team clearly defined
Process for end-to-end testing life cycle defined and implemented
Changes to technical tasks or estimates handled by a defined process
Requirements change process defined
Entrance and exit criteria for testing documented
Availability of a project level defect management process
Availability of communication plan process

Metrics

Documents and tracks schedule commitments
Estimates and tracks level of effort
Documents and tracks service levels with upstream and downstream groups
Aware of test organization goals
Tracks performance against test organization goals
Aware of division level goals
Tracks performance of division level goals
Test metrics collected, analyzed, and reported
Understands the business impacts of schedule delays
Understands business impacts of escaped defects

Training

Team is trained in lean methods

Tools and Automation

Availability of test management tools
Availability of process for test automation

By now you are probably getting the sense that either quality processes are very important to lean and agile transformation processes, or that the transformation in this example is for that of a quality department. Both answers are correct. In a business process transformation project quality programs are essential in order to assure success, and many of the quality behaviors are the first practices to disappear as organizations move to lean or agile. The Four Spheres Model of Agile and Lean Transformation element of Assessing Readiness is one of the prime movers to ensure any organization is capable and prepared to support thriving agile and lean processes and teams.

Assessing Readiness

Tracking the quality behaviors and their lean and agile counterpart practices are essential to effective implementation. Another key relationship to understand is the close relationship between agile and lean methods. Agile can easily be viewed as a lean software development practice (see Figure 5.3).

With the two programs being closely related, completing the assessment of agile and lean readiness together simply makes the process of finding the readiness gaps a little quicker and provides for some cross-over in the analysis. Projects were chosen for inclusion in the readiness assessment based on very simple criteria. The project had to be completed within the last 90 days, or currently ongoing during the assessment. Team members from the projects and the project managers were chosen as the participants for the assessment. The assessment questions were delivered to the respondents as a questionnaire to ensure that the respondent was able to ask for clarification. In this way we were able to ensure that the answers we received were complete and truly represented the state of the project.

In completing the readiness assessment, our goal was not simply the collection of data. Nor was the goal the comparison of one project to another, but rather the desire to find gaps in our ability to support agile and lean methods. We needed to determine where we should focus our attention in the implementation of new methods and to develop a solid change management plan that would target our weaknesses and aid us in spreading around those practices that were already in place and maturing. In order to accomplish this, the analysis needs to provide a quickly digestible, graphical presentation of both strengths and weaknesses that an executive can use to focus resources, and a manager may use to target change.

Heat maps provide just the right mix between usable data and fast-focus acquisition. Graphically, the weaknesses are depicted in red and the strengths in green indicating those areas where further investigation and potential

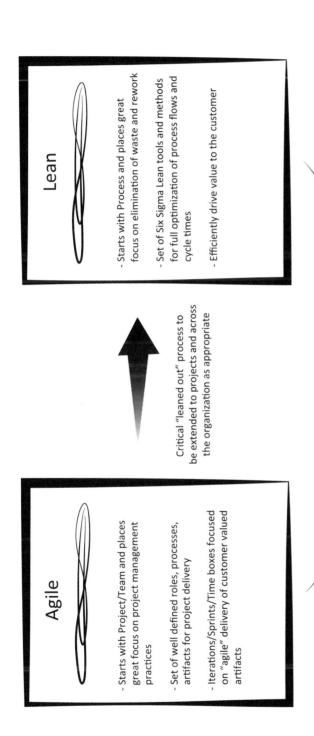

Agile

- Starts with Project/Team and places great focus on project management practices

- Set of well defined roles, processes, artifacts for project delivery

- Iterations/Sprints/Time boxes focused on "agile" delivery of customer valued artifacts

Critical "leaned out" process to be extended to projects and across the organization as appropriate

Lean

- Starts with Process and places great focus on elimination of waste and rework

- Set of Six Sigma Lean tools and methods for full optimization of process flows and cycle times

- Efficiently drive value to the customer

Shared Values and Fundamentals

Voice of Customer—Customer Value

Voice of Business—Cycle Time and Efficiency

Proven industry wide methodologies

Figure 5.3   Relationship between agile and lean

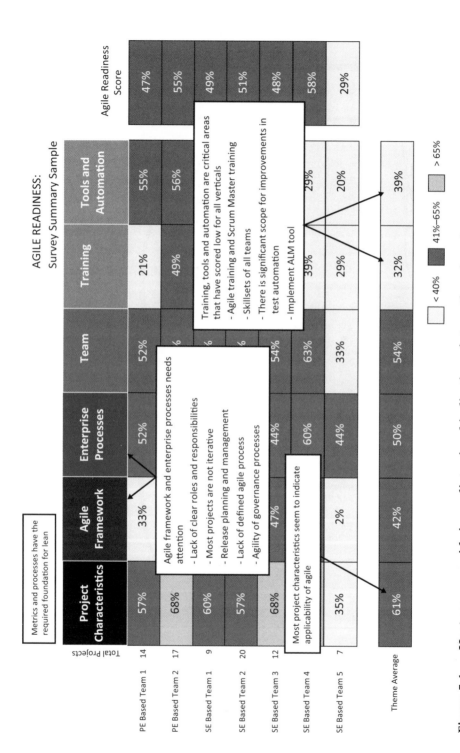

AGILE READINESS:
Survey Summary Sample

Total Projects		Project Characteristics	Agile Framework	Enterprise Processes	Team	Training	Tools and Automation	Agile Readiness Score
14	PE Based Team 1	57%	33%	52%	52%	21%	55%	47%
17	PE Based Team 2	68%		52%		49%	56%	55%
9	SE Based Team 1	60%						49%
20	SE Based Team 2	57%						51%
12	SE Based Team 3	68%	47%	44%	54%			48%
	SE Based Team 4			60%	63%	39%	29%	58%
7	SE Based Team 5	35%	2%	44%	33%	29%	20%	29%
	Theme Average	61%	42%	50%	54%	32%	39%	

Metrics and processes have the required foundation for lean

Agile framework and enterprise processes needs attention
- Lack of clear roles and responsibilities
- Most projects are not iterative
- Release planning and management
- Lack of defined agile process
- Agility of governance processes

Training, tools and automation are critical areas that have scored low for all verticals
- Agile training and Scrum Master training
- Skillsets of all teams
- There is significant scope for improvements in test automation
- Implement ALM tool

Most project characteristics seem to indicate applicability of agile

□ < 40%   ■ 41%–65%   ▦ > 65%

Figure 5.4   Heat maps provide immediate visual indication of strength and weakness

improvement projects are to begin. Keep in mind that a an area of weakness is likely expected: however, the heat maps provide the ability for the executives, whom may have only seconds of opportunity to focus on the problem and make a decision, to understand both the geography and depth of the situation (see Figure 5.4).

Data for the heat map comes from the answers to each of the research questions, and are calculated simply as the percent of positive response to a given question. Information is presented on a by project basis in order that the investigation of the strengths and weaknesses are easily identified providing quick response in sharing effective practices. Areas of green should be investigated such that an area of maturity can be understood in depth and evaluated for possible cross pollination of project teams currently working in an agile or lean program.

Areas of red, or weakness, are not necessarily to be defined as a problem. This could simply be an indication that the project team has not yet been exposed to the lean or agile practices. When looking at Figure 5.4 we can easily see that the project titled "PE Based Team 2" reflects green under the element title Project Characteristics in our agile heat map, and yet shows yellow in the areas of "Training" and "Tools and Automation."

As a leader, the first response would be to follow up with the team manager to determine if team members may perhaps require more training, or if the problem is simply one of awareness or desire for greater information and experience. What may be of greater concern is the project titled "SE Based Team 3" where the indication is that of an agile project, and yet less than half the respondents indicate the project is using a well-defined agile framework. Upon further investigation the leadership discovered the team expressed a lack of clearly defined and unique roles and responsibilities and lack of release planning. Problems such as these may warrant more intervention on the part of leadership. As the leadership team takes a step back to look at the bigger picture it becomes clear that a focus on broader training opportunities may be warranted with less than 40 percent of the project team members reported being exposed to agile training and tools. Choosing the right methods for the right problem is often times confusing and fraught with a multitude of voices shouting in the dark to follow and adopt the latest trend in quick hit problem-solving techniques. Often leaders will punt the problem to the consultants. In the Management Governance sphere of the Four Spheres Model of Agile and Lean Transformation selecting the right approach offers a decision model that cuts through the haze and provides fool proof selection model to follow.

Selecting the Approach

Choosing the right project and the right project methodologies can be a problem as the leadership team moves to address some of the more immediate weaknesses. Understanding when the expense of detailed data investigation and problem definition is the key to success and when a team should be capable of fully understanding the resolution and just get the change in place can save a great deal of time and money. In Figure 5.5 we can see the progression from detailed investigation and complexity to "Just Do It" projects that move from the definition of the effort to the implementation of the outcome with little governance in between.

Projects are characterized by the degree to which the problem and the solution are known and widely accepted by leadership as such. These are the problems with which employees and team members are continuously and intimately involved on a daily basis. Problems such as these tend to be less complex, although the implementation may be somewhat time consuming and perhaps resource intensive. Problems that may fall into this area are topics such as time reporting or defect management. These are problems that are often grown out a series of process changes or perhaps the combining of several departments during reorganization and therefore the intermingling of organizational cultures and tools.

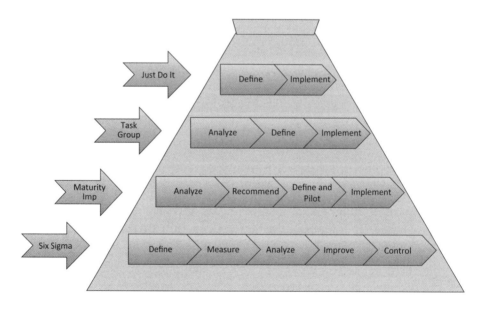

Figure 5.5   Project complexity and governance

As the organization changes tools are often combined into a system that may result in redundant reporting of defects in multiple places or perhaps the dual reporting of personnel time in multiple collection tools to provide for both project tracking and capital management by the finance department. Employees, team members, and leaders all recognize the problem and the impact of the problem on the organization and often realize the solution is likely bridging of the technology gap. Developers likely already know the solution and are ready with a technology fix and stand ready to make and complete the implementation. This is a "Just Do It" problem simply waiting for the go ahead to complete the work and plan the implementation strategy.

Moving deeper into more complex issues we enter into a problem where the definition is well known and often a continuous irritant to the team, and yet how to resolve the issue is still an unknown, or at least not agreed. These problems often mascaraed as "Just Do It" projects. At times an example of this could be the building of the technology bridge between time or defect reporting tools to reduce the amount of redundant entries a team must make on a daily basis. If, however, the solution is not agreed due to deeper technology issues or even the simple politics of cultural gaps in the newly formed organization, a greater level of investigation may be needed to come to agreement on the solution definition. In this case a team may be formed to investigate the feasibility and necessity of the project and to ponder and vet the proposal for potential solution. This team would be expected to mentor and facilitate the build out of the solution and the implementation and institutionalization of the chosen solution.

In the next two levels of the pyramid the projects become more complex and reach deeper into the daily operations and maturity of the process definition. Projects chosen at this level are designed to move the operational processes of the organization upward in whatever maturity model the leadership has chosen to manage. At this level the processes are defined and measured. The measures are then continuously reviewed and tracked on a daily basis, on a daily basis if necessary based on the volatility of the metrics, and subjected to a process of continuous improvement. Processes in this level of improvement are to be mapped using a lean value stream effort and non-value added activities removed to ensure the process is refined and refocused on the customer's expectations of quality.

In the base layer of the pyramid we find the complex projects. Those projects to which the leadership, employees, and team leaders have an awareness that something is wrong, that something or some activity within the process is not fulfilling the need or expectation of management and causing the end product to miss the mark, are launched at the base of the pyramid. Projects launched at the base of the pyramid do not have a previously known problem statement or solution definition, but rather a problem that must be discovered and validated before an analysis and solution team may be gathered and chartered. These projects are always complex and often cross-organizational and must be facilitated by trained and knowledgeable practitioners of Six Sigma or lean or perhaps another well respected problem-solving methodology. It is imperative that these teams also work in a way that compliments the agile and lean methodology that the organization has espoused.

The selection process, when choosing projects and chartering teams needs to take into account the complexity of the issue (see Figure 5.6). By following the Four Quadrant Project Chartering Guide, the complexity of the project selection and facilitation problems in the previous paragraphs are made clear. Each of the four quadrants is used as a facilitation tool to ensure the right problem-solving method is chosen for the right type of issue. In the final quadrant of the Four Quadrant Project Chartering Guide, the problem is noted as being Unknown, and yet the solution is identified as Known. This condition is well known to quality practitioners. What often happens during a process improvement or change program is the classic *solution searching for a problem* paradigm. In this case the solution is shopped like a carnival barker, standing at the front of their booth with a solution in hand and waved overhead shouting to the crowds the glories and benefits one may quickly attain if they would only step forward and take part in their wonder filled journey. The solution, they will tell you, is at hand should they only choose to take part in their pet project. All too often the carnival barker will find a manager willing to carry the solution forward as a project. A gray empty box appears in the bottom right corner of Figure 5.6, for this is what the managers will receive in the end if they carry forth with the *solution looking for a problem* project; gray emptiness. Any known solution offered as the resolution to an unknown problem needs to be carried back to the team for greater evaluation, for it is likely centered on a hunch with little understanding of the underlying cause and effect relationship.

As the governance team moves through the project selection process, it is critical to maintain a focus on the heat maps. Target the weaknesses and spread the faith regarding the strengths. Where the weakness of one team aligns with the strength of another is where the Known Problems align with the Known Solutions. Bring these teams together for training opportunities to allow the subject matter experts to share their knowledge and have these teams document

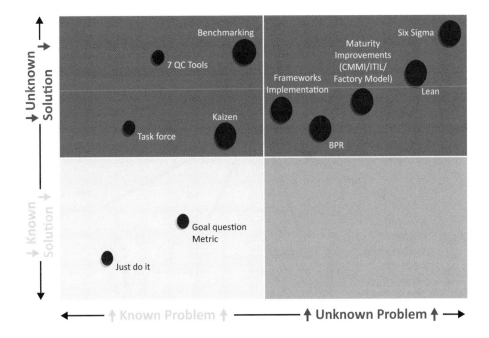

Figure 5.6   Four quadrant project chartering guide

the knowledge to ensure the tribal knowledge one finds in successful teams can be replicated throughout the larger organization.

Areas of weakness across many teams without any one team scoring high and measured green in the heat map may be an area that likely falls into the known problem without a known solution. The top left quadrant shown in Figure 5.6 may be a problem that is readily resolved using a benchmarking trip to a well-known and respected organization within your company, or perhaps a strategic partner. If in the case of a gap in training or missing tools, this may be readily resolved using a panel of subject matter experts and members of the training department of tools development team to identify a solution that works well within the culture and working methods of the team.

Remembering the customer during the governance process can be tricky as teams plunge forward with the agile and lean build out of new processes. While both methodologies are customer centric, the problem comes in the solution selection. Teams and leaders may have a tendency to believe they know what is best for the customer. While this may be true in some cases, it is important to at least take a look at ways in which the customer's perspective may be accounted in the process. Asking the questions will sometimes suffice

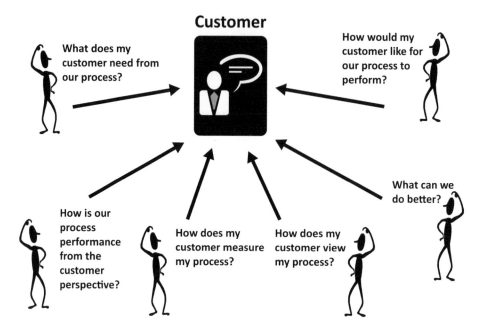

Figure 5.7   Solutions need to account for the customer

when building the process and the means by which measures are reviewed. Many of the answers to these questions are found in the Unknown Problem and Unknown-Solution quadrant of our chart. These questions can have some challenges in determining the where and how to gather information as many agile and lean methodology teams are deeply imbedded in the engineering divisions of most organizations.

When the teams don't have clear lines of communication with the customer, as is likely the case, the team must reach out to the business side of the organization, namely marketing, for it is here that the customer-business relationships are built and monitored. Data exists and can be readily mined for nuggets or jewels of information that can make the agile and lean implementation shine, and the entire process feel successful at the end. This data is essential in identifying the right problems and critical in identifying an effective solution.

Any work undertaken to fill the gaps needs to be addressed; however, there may be gaps that are less apparent when looking at building out a governance process. Cultural and trust elements are every bit as important as tools and training. Having a strategy in place that addresses the challenges of virtuality in the work place that includes the differences and the likenesses is an essential tool in our work belt. The Four Spheres Model of Agile and Lean Transformation offers a clear cut path for building that strategy.

Team Governance Strategy

In working with projects in a global project environment, leadership confidence and skill in the establishment of trust with and by leaders can be critical to reducing the risks caused by several aspects of working offshore that are not present in the relatively homogeneous environment of in-house, face-to-face, project teams. In order to address the needs of global project integration, effective communications and information discovery using application of technology and leadership has become a key element in project management (Anantatmula and Thomas, 2010).

Technology allows for the lifting of barriers that restricted traditional jobs. Barriers such as geographic boundaries, cultural norms, and organizational practices and restrictions regarding the timing and the locations of employee contributions no longer limit how work gets done. As we explore the relationship between technology, motivation, and teamwork among software and systems developers, engineers, and testers and other quality professionals, an understanding of the team dynamics of motivation, communications, and belonging are highly relevant as these processes are the key elements in the needed governance.

To help us understand the needs of the new team dynamics of a twenty-first century project team, Duarte and Snyder (2006) provide a seven factor framework with which to address the conversation regarding management strategy and potential team success in virtual teams. According to Duarte and Snyder the seven critical elements of a virtual team strategy are:

1. Human resource policy.

2. Training.

3. Processes.

4. Collaboration and communication mediation.

5. Culture.

6.   Leadership support.

7.   Leadership and membership competency.

These seven elements, when plans are formulated with policies that accommodate the needs of virtual teams and virtual team leadership, may provide greater success in managing the global workforce. With the elements of an effective strategy built into the tactical project planning of the organization we can find support among complimentary studies that will help managers formulate a strategy that is customized to fit your particular project and environmental needs.

Human Resource Policy

The practice of quality in IT and information systems (IS) has evolved from one of an engineering focus in feature and requirement verification, to one requiring membership with and participation in engineering and development practitioner teams. While this shift may seem natural to some, it does come with some new and difficult challenges in human resource management practice. In the past, IT and IS employees were considered to be motivated by their passion for their craft. With a shift to virtual team-based planning and execution of projects, the silent individual must now become a member of a larger execution model.

We have talked about team-based practices and the relationship between teams and agile or lean methods, but here we will take a somewhat different approach to the subject. The discussion regarding motivation of employees is extremely important to the topic of empowerment and the freedom solid human resource policy plays in creating an environment that motivates the employee to participate. In an article a few years back, Faircloth and Hamm recorded their studies of the motivation to achieve high marks in school in a group of high school students noting that membership, or as we have described it as identification of oneself with the group, as a significant variable in defining the relationship between motivation and achievement (2005).

Trust has always been an essential part of teambuilding, and yet we are really only learning how working in a small world environment may affect team dynamics. This new team model shrinks our view of the world and expands our view of the team thus impacting the essentiality of trust in team dynamics as teams begin to rely more heavily on geographically dispersed team membership in building effective communications. Agility, on the other hand, is often considered to be challenged in this small world environment due to the inherent or assumed reliance on face-to-face project teams, but with the proper human resource policy in place these challenges can be readily overcome. We all know the challenges.

Members are left out of planning meetings and daily scrums or standups when they are not immediately available. This can be due to the feelings of urgency team members face when making project commitments and the pressures placed on them to perform in short project time space such as two-week sprints. Human resource policy is uniquely positioned to address these issues in planning a strong and robust work-home life policy. As these issues of timing and stress are worked out for agile methods, team members feel the relief and freedom to plan effectively. Freedom to express their work in useful and relevant sprints will release the teams and allow them to open the team to the extended membership rosters necessary to accept the small world programs necessary for virtual team memberships.

Feeling at ease within the group and at home with the role we play is necessary to building membership, and may be in some part supported and driven by equitable management policy decisions. Ryan and Kossek express this concept as an essential part of the human resource plan by saying that, to the degree that management may implement policy that eases the work and home life stressors, then employees may move toward feelings of membership within the work group (2008). The real question that comes to mind for all of us is "What does that look like in practice?"

The easiest answer is to express this in terms of what it does not look like. Developers, when working in an agile team, are asked to create their own timelines as they draw down work from the project backlog; however, almost every team will assume that a sprint is to be no more than two weeks no matter the work. Not all work fits in the two-week sprint and yet the project team will undoubtedly insist the team member commit to a two-week production cycle. When we worked in the financial industry our team was trained in waterfall methods, but during a merger we suddenly found ourselves in an agile environment, and during the initial stages of this merger fell prey to just this behavior.

Our team members did not know how to push back on the time commitments and in an effort to fit in and please the new boss accepted the demand for two-week sprints. Team members began to work up to 24-days, several days a week. Their health suffered and so did their families as they struggled to keep up with the commitments and those that could not were asked to leave. People would arrive at work with eyes dark and saggy and feet shuffling across the tiled floors like B-movie zombies, moaning and groaning as they took their place to begin work again. Mistakes happened and rework piled up as milestones were missed. Our lean processes unraveled and team agility and flexibility failed as managers felt compelled to step and implement the old standby transactional management techniques to drive the work load toward completion to save the go-live dates.

Building a human resource strategy that prevents these artificial stressors and allows the team the freedom they need to plan realistic target dates and maintain their quality of life is an essential element of the agile implementation strategy. Additionally, to the degree that managers may equitably implement these policies, this may in part have an effect on the degree to which employees may perceive themselves to be a member of the organization or team, and feed team performance through higher levels of trust and commitment (Park et al., 2005).

Performance, according to Whetten and Cameron (1995), is a quotient of ability and motivation, and ability the quotient of aptitude, training, and resources, while motivation the quotient of desire and commitment. These five human resource variables come together to make the backbone of every project team, with the capability of impacting the likelihood of the team's success or failure. When we talk about our agile project teams in the context of their ability to get the work done the idea of an effective human resource policy begins to take shape in the context of aptitude, training, and resources. As we build out our project team we need to look to whether we have established our project teams with team members that have the basic elements necessary to focus on the work at hand and the natural capacity to fulfill the needs of the team.

As we look at the list and the elements of team member ability it is interesting to note that the two of the key elements are leadership issues and not necessarily the responsibility of the employee. Training and resources, or rather the lack of these elements, are never the responsibility of the employee or team members. Leaders are expected to evaluate their team against the functions and deliverables of the project team and make an early and well-planned determination of the training the project team may require and any new resources in tools or knowledge they may need to acquire.

NTCP Diamond Analysis

One easy method of making this determination is to look at the work of Shenhar and Divr (2007) as they described the NTCP diamond analysis process. Using the diamond analysis, the project leaders evaluate the project using a spider diagram with the X and Y axis labeled on the four points with Technology at the top, Novelty to the right, Pace at the bottom, and Complexity to the left. When talking about training needs, however, it is the Technology and Novelty discussions that become relevant. As technology changes increase, and with new or breakthrough changes are desired, so does the need for new skills and perhaps training.

The Technology axis is hash marked with titles of low-tech, medium-tech, high-tech, and super-high-tech to provide a visual for the project leaders as an indicator of the degree to which technology may be a factor in project planning. As the project moves up the scale toward super-high-tech the leaders for the project must make a detailed analysis regarding the ability of the team to fulfill the mission. Training or perhaps resourcing the team through skills augmentation such as new team members may be required to meet the project deadlines and technology expectations.

A high level of Novelty in the project will require similar analysis. This axis is hash marked with a scale that reads Derivative, Platform, and Breakthrough to indicate the degree to which the functions or products delivered in this project may be new and innovative. As the project slides out on the axis toward breakthrough, project team may require new team members, or perhaps the availability of new resources in the form of tools, computer hardware, or even access to a new skills pool in the form of new business partners which often leads to a virtual work relationship where one did not exist in the past. As you may well realize, at any time "new" is the key word in any project team discussion the team may become both highly interested and threatened by the project at the same time.

Novelty and new will almost always create mixed emotions in the work place. They are words that drive technology workers frantic with interesting challenges and drive the creative juices and then at the same time lift the fears of failure and inadequacy. Making this adjustment may create new stresses and new threats to the team and require a high level of both self-awareness and leadership. This requires us to focus somewhat lower on the natural order of things as Maslow stated in his early writing.

Virtuality

Virtuality, according to Ahuja (2010), is the new norm as organizations diversify across geographic boundaries, therefore straining the corporate ability to maintain a focus on the motivational factors in Whetten and Cameron's performance equation. Pre-dating Whetten and Cameron and establishing a foundation for the desire factor within Whetten and Cameron's equation, Maslow (1948) provides motivational theory in a graphical representation of unsatisfied needs in a hierarchical pyramid based on the human desire to satisfy those needs of the most basic level prior to graduation up the hierarchy. Physiological and safety needs, according to Maslow, must be satisfied before the employee is driven toward satisfaction of needs at the social and self-esteem levels (1948).

At the pinnacle of Maslow's hierarchy of motivational needs is the desire for self-actualization as the employee seeks to reach their full potential driven by intrinsic needs for satisfaction, as the employee's need in health, safety, bonding, and respect are met (Maslow, 1948). Herzberg compliments with the theory of hygiene factors[2] in motivational theory seeking to explain the demotivation, or stepping down Maslow's hierarchy, as lower-level needs are raised regarding self-esteem, and social needs (1965; 1948). With this said, human resource managers need to establish policies that support the basic needs, and establish policy that allows for greater motivation in personal and career growth to support the increasing motivational needs of their personnel.

Once effective policies are in place, they must be institutionalized in such a way as to inform and support the project team. Equity in the way in which the information is shared, and opportunity is provided, however, is essential in maintaining what is gained through the establishment of these policies. If in fact the policies exist that provide opportunity for training as an example, removal of such an opportunity, or unreasonably difficult access to the training may become what Herzberg describes as a hygiene issue.

---

2   Herzberg proposed hygiene factors known as the Two-Factor Theory as a way of describing the need to maintain opportunity within the work place such as the pursuit of higher order needs in Maslow's Hierarchy of Needs theory of motivation. At its most basic level, Herzberg's Two-Factor theory may be described to say an opportunity is a motivator as long as it has real potential to be fulfilled, and once fulfilled it then is no longer a motivational factor, and may soon become a demotivator if a new opportunity for fulfillment is not represented in its place.

Training and Development

Maslow and Herzberg form a solid basis for further understanding of employee motivational research in the twenty-first century as managers seek to understand motivational theory in relation to their virtual project teams. Herzberg's assertion that the personal rewards provided by the meaningfulness of the employee's work contribution plays heavily in the equation regarding motivational theory and the virtual project team (1965). Contributing to this conversation, Blaskova (2009) exclaims that team member motivation is often formed intrinsically through a worker's internal belief system.

Workers, Blaskova continues, are willing to adjust their performance based on the presence of motivational factors in the work place, which during times of economic challenges such as those facing managers in the twenty-first century are often difficult to provide (2009). As companies look for ways to respond to the changes demanded by the small world economy, and seek ways to address the financial difficulties that this creates, maintaining a motivational work place is becoming more difficult as teams become increasingly geographically dispersed. As purses are tightened in the face of economic uncertainty, employees are challenged with potential concerns regarding employment security at the lower social and safety needs of Maslow's pyramid (1948).

Powell (2000) expressed this concern declaring that as teams move to the virtual team model, socialization of teams is often reduced by the feeling of separation, hindering the establishment of support and membership that employees once gained through work place relationships. Managers need to find ways in which rewards are maintained as budgets decline. One way in which we have seen companies make this shift is through creative use of training opportunities.

As managers do, we have had many talks with peers throughout the financial, political, and nuclear power industries. Everyone is struggling with the same challenges. How to stretch the training dollars and maintain an environment that allows for creativity and opportunity in the work force? Many managers are training new subject matter experts (SMEs) on a needed topic, and including training and mentorship on how to train their peers on the subject. These newly trained trainers are then offered the opportunity to provide a free lunch for everyone that comes to their training session.

Opening these presentation opportunities to employees and team members with little experience can inadvertently back fire on the management team through increased stress and fear among a workforce not accustomed to public speaking. Be aware that this will indeed create both a new set of rewards and opportunity as well as a new set of stresses. Counter this problem and head it off before it occurs. We did this through the creativity of one of our employees who, through his own creativity, developed a local on-site speaker's development program. These organizations are not new and provide solid information in public speaking that would welcome the chance to expand their reach with great training and reading materials available online.

Our company now has a few chapters in different locations to help employees develop their skills in speaking and training that will both develop new career opportunities for them and new training skills for us. As is often the usual development in the work place, what is old becomes what is new. Companies are going back to the days of the total quality management (TQM) craze in order to find new ways to motivate teams through process change as well. Quality Circles are formed to find ways to stretch their metaphorical envelope and build in new motivational opportunities. Employee teams, using employee formed leadership opportunities, are able to use their own creativity to improve how they get work done, develop new processes, and train their peers, allowing for greater opportunity in the higher tears of Maslow's hierarchy.

Leadership Support of Virtual Teams

Zigurs describes the complexity of leadership in a virtual setting to the degree to which the team is virtual (2003). As more elements of virtuality are added to the team dynamics, the greater the complexity of leadership issues the team may face. Complicating the issues in team complexity for leaders is the issues in team dynamics as members come and go within the team depending upon the work in progress, and changes in project goals and requirements, as well as the necessity for team member autonomy is a virtual setting. Additionally, traditional challenges such as monitoring team progress, providing feedback, and resolving conflicts become greater challenges when working apart from the team.

A natural difference between virtual teams and traditional teams is not simply the physical separation, but the additional challenge of the psychological dispersion. Leaders need new skills in this environment. They become facilitators rather than directive, and encouragers rather than managers (DeRosa, Hantula, Kock, and D'Arcy, 2004). These new skills may threaten less experienced managers, and will likely require new training opportunities to help managers cope with the lack of control a virtual environment offers to the management ranks.

Self-identification and categorization as a leader, possibly even more so than as a member of a group, is made more difficult when separation from a group may cause a leader to feel some level of competition for control. Managers that rely upon transactional behaviors as well as those that prefer transformational leadership styles may also face greater challenges in this setting depending upon the degree to which the team may work virtually. Executives likely find this unusual that lower-level leaders will struggle with the concept of competing for control of their work environments as this is a common occurrence that the executive level. For the project manager, this concept is very unsettling and can add to their feelings of mistrust and insecurity.

Transactional management styles rely upon the exchange of action and reward, or perhaps management by exception, while transformation leaders may prefer forms of inspiration and extrinsic motivations to move team members to greater levels of performance (Hambley, O'Neill, and Kline, 2007). Both styles may be effective, and possibly dependent upon the degree to which teams may operative autonomously. As Spillane (2005) noted, the degree to which autonomy is necessary may increase the need for the distribution of leadership roles to ensure effective team performance. The needs of the team at a point in the project, and possibly the degree to which the diffusion of leadership roles is necessary, may have an impact on which leadership style is effective at any given time.

As Hambley et al. describe the changes in leadership based on situational awareness, teams need different kinds of leaders as the focus of the work shifts (2007). Teams working in more creative roles at some point in the project may need a transformational leader to inspire greater levels of creative thinking and idea development. As the project shifts to a greater level of technical difficulty and engineering functions may be better led by leaders with transactional skills. Short-term, fast-acting, high-performance teams may feel unfairly intruded upon by leaders that inspire to lead teams to greater levels of performance.

This too may be sorted out with the help of the NTCP chart presented by Shenhar and Divr in 2007. As the project lead evaluates the project regarding the degree to which technology and novelty require high levels of freedom and creativity, or whether the schedule (pace) or a high level of complexity will require greater degrees of transactional leadership, the project leads and management team can determine the level to which they must be directly in control of the project. Providing tools such as the NTCP analysis will aid managers and leaders alike in making leadership style decisions, and the all-important decision regarding which leaders are best suited for which projects and project team needs.

Team Collaboration Mediation

Moore (2007) addresses the issue of the psychology of team socialization indicating the need for leadership motivational practices, such as goal setting, personnel development, and activity coordination, is absolutely essential in strengthening virtual, geographically dispersed, teams. Having to work through technologies such as web messaging, text, email, and other forms of communication interventions, Moore suggests that team leaders be required to have the skill sets to build the relationships between team members, create the psychologically safe work environment, and provide encouragement and opportunity for professional growth (2007). In virtual team settings, even more so than in traditional teams, team autonomy may have a greater impact on team collaboration than does the presentation of specific technology.

Peters and Manz (2007) suggest that moving from a traditionally regimented leadership style to that of diffused leadership may provide greater opportunity for collaboration due to the level of freedom this style provides. As teams feel free to experiment and make decisions, they may feel greater empowerment to express their ideas and therefore discuss the opportunity that different options may provide. The technology therefore is a necessary enabling element, but not necessarily a driver of virtual team collaboration.

Peters and Manz suggest that virtual team collaboration, like that of the more traditional face-to-face project team, may be defined by the degree to which team members may share influence and support, as well as participation in team decisions and outcomes. This includes activities such as shared conflict resolution, creativity and experimentation, and the ability to affect direct communication and participation in such events. Team support, conflict, innovation and creativity, and experimentation are all heavily influenced by the depth of the relationships that team members may build within their virtual environment.

Organizational Culture

Team socialization, according to Moore (2007), is a required motivational tool that must be provided. This is accomplished, according to Moore, most effectively in face-to-face communications, and at minimum on an intermittent schedule, to address the needs that Maslow (1948) described for social level actualization before a team can attain greater satisfaction and motivation (2007). Managers of effective virtual teams rely heavily on understanding the feelings, work problems, issues, and other situational conditions, as well as individual motivations and team member interdependencies to demonstrate situational awareness and empathy for team members. Additionally, the necessity to listen attentively and in a non-evaluative way is heightened due to the absence of face-to-face communications.

As companies adjust to allow for decentralization of some decision-making, and change reporting structures to make communications more direct, companies are finding that changing the culture of the company can at times require changes in the way the company hierarchy is formed. Many companies, Peters and Manz contend, will go so far as to formally change from a hierarchical management structure to a flat and open company structure (2007). The authors state that as the reporting structure is changed to allow for diffusion in decision-making and leadership responsibilities changes, so does the culture of the company.

This works in both large and small organizations. My department contains only three full time employees, and a handful of consultants, and yet even with such a small group we work in a diffused leadership style. Although we all talk multiple times each day, and when we say talk, we include text, email, instant messaging (IM), and phone, as well as intermittent face to face, each person is empowered, and yes encouraged, to make their own decisions. My role is that of facilitator to help make their vision within their own zone of control and responsibility to take shape. We simply provide the needed guidance to help my talented team move in the same direction, and form a consistent and cohesive program.

In an environment with multiple international cultures this can be a bit more challenging, and yet diffused leadership and flat organizational structures can be effective. Once again within my small group we do reflect an international strategy. At least half of my team is offshore, and another third is half way across the United States from the remainder of the team. We exist within three time zones every day, and yet work all problems in a collaborative environment that includes multiple organizations with every discussion.

Having team members that have the experience working with multiple cultures does help. The company needs to be aware that multiple cultures exist in every project, and provide the training and monitoring to ensure the work environment remains sensitive to the needs of these work teams. We make sure to ask about holiday schedules when deliverables are requested, and work to ensure we schedule meeting times that are fair and reasonable across the time zones. Cultural awareness needs to be built into the team's charter and supported by company policies wherever necessary.

Standardized Policy and Procedures

Improving team performance may be accomplished by providing teams with an easy way to improve communications, and clarifying roles and expectations while giving teams a means of implementing a lateral structure in project teams (Wong and Burton, 2000). Therefore, as Weems-Landingham points out, the manager of work teams must enlist a multitude of media in employing effective, participative listening (2004). Managers must seek to understand the facts in conflict resolution and coaching events, and draw accurate and complete representations of factual events (Turner, 1999). These simple practices provide a means of ensuring equitable policy application, as well as employing the traditional methods of empathy, teambuilding, and participation to bridge the geographic gap and encourage self-identification with core team membership.

Text messaging, IM, email, and other electronic media are generally considered to be effective and essential communications devices and strategies for effective work teams. Using multiple communication channels are necessary and may be effective, but should never be the singular means of communication and team socialization. Face to face is always necessary and should be worked into the schedule on a regular basis. Within the use of effective communications media must also be the message of equitable application of policy and procedure to reinforce member trust among the team and with the corporation.

Further, standardization of policies and procedures will help team members to become acclimated to a project very quickly. As teams learn what is expected of them on a project, these expectations will easily translate into rapid team formation on the next big project. This further reinforces membership in a project setting, and provides a line of sight for team members to a much longer horizon to their work relationships.

Team Leader and Team Member Competency

Trust building may take on a calculative nature as opposed to normative as a means of accommodating political differences (Mizrachi et al., 2007). The effective manager of high-performing teams, therefore, needs to find creative ways to fill the needs of the employee in safety and socialization if the team is to be a truly effective workforce. As Herzberg points out, a base element in effecting a satisfying job experience is recognizing those aspects of the employee's work that achieve goals and milestones, as well as the basics of the job requirements in a consistent and effective daily manner (1965).

This may require a new set of management competencies. Competencies are those skills or behaviors that would be agreed to be core to the capability of a group or company to compete in their chosen market. Skills such as the ability to build trust or create a learning organization would be new core competencies needed on the management team of a face-to-face or virtual project organization (Holton, 2001). Other areas of competency that will need to be established are those of team building and group dynamics, conflict resolution, and group communication.

In teams that may be include the virtual elements such as diffusion across time zones and cultures the added competencies of cross-cultural communication, process facilitation, and creating and sustaining remote team work will be needed (Holten, 2001). Hertel, Geister, and Konradt break the discussion of competencies into three general categories of cognitive, task oriented, and teamwork related socio-emotional (2005). Attributes such as conscientiousness and integrity cooperativeness, along with solid communication skills and self-management, become essential in both management and employee level participants in any project environment, and most importantly in a virtual environment.

Integrating a Virtual Team Management Strategy That Will be the Most Effective for Managing Information Technology Development Projects

An integrated strategy should impact each of the seven factors described by Duarte and Snyder (2006), and therefore each is addressed in the following paragraphs. Management strategy must be organized such that it draws the employee to the organization, fostering commitment, and fulfilling the expectations of the employee engendering trust, openness, and a high level of participation (Kanter, 1968; Zand, 1972). It must be open and participative, allowing for the need of an autonomous element and leadership opportunity, and provide a collaborative environment that encourages synchronous planning and regular closed loop communications utilizing effectively integrated technologies.

Processes should be developed that are based around how work gets done, and supports the remote team members need for participation and collaboration. Remote team members need to feel that their voice is heard, and their needs are accounted for on a daily basis. The perception, as well as the reality, of collaboration and membership in geographically dispersed teams is essential to the ability to build team effectiveness and performance. We say this in this backward fashion for a purpose. Team members working remotely or in a virtual setting need to feel and understand that their voice is heard. Just because the reality may be that their needs have been accounted in the process does not mean that they may well understand this reality.

Attempting to incorporate the needs of virtual team members, if not managed well, can also be an impediment in enacting effective technology. This may occur in situations where one or more groups are at odds regarding goals, or conflicting social norms. This situation may be aggravated in situations where, as Schwarz and Watson point out, management is in disagreement with other employee groups or IT implementation teams (2005).

While this may sound odd or even contrived, we have often seen technology decisions made to satisfy management desires rather than the needs of the virtual team members. Simple technologies like defect management for IT projects can either support the needs of the virtual team members in information discovery, or serve to aggravate their feelings of membership. We have seen cases where a project team working across work teams at the program level struggle to work in a virtual manner because their request to combine defect management instances of the same tool were ignored. The team members repeatedly requested multiple teams to combine their use of the defect management tool to allow them to better understand the data in a project.

The teams were forced to spend hours attempting to pull information from the tool from multiple instances and combine the data using spreadsheets in order to be able to report on the project progress. To successfully accomplish this, the team had to put one person on data collection and reporting full time. Requests such as this would seem to be simple; however, we saw in one case where the discussion lasted for years.

While the team members continued to struggle in finding and aggregating project information managers continued to argue about their desire for technological freedom to work in a way that was best for their own needs rather than finding a way to accommodate the needs of those working virtually on the team program. This can occur with time tracking, just as easily if multiple instances of the same tool are used in different ways across programs. While these examples may be simple, they do affect perceptions of membership within the team.

HUMAN RESOURCE POLICY

Sarker et al. (2003) and Mizrachi et al. (2007) each discuss at length the need for equitable application of policies and procedures, and the expectation that such policy will consistently provide an environment with little ambiguity regarding organizational goals. Building a participative and open organizational policy requires the active management of knowledge and policy, and successful implementation of a participative policy requires the active participation of all members of the organization up and down the hierarchy (Ardichvili, Page, and Wentling, 2003).

Participation, Ardichvili et al. (2003) found, rises from a belief that sharing furthers the greater good of the whole. With this in mind, as policy is seen as equitable and flexible, and as managers seek to bring about fairness and reasonableness regarding home and work life balance, employees identify with a policy of inclusiveness. As employees feel that their voice is heard and their participation has made a difference in corporate policy, they may be more inclined to participate and share in the greater good of the organization, and commit themselves to the success of the whole (Ryan and Kossek, 2008).

Policies that commit to the employee a desire to implement programs that support participation may also feed into the discussion regarding motivational strategies espoused by Maslow and Herzberg. As employees participate in building effective human resource policy that includes an understanding of a virtual work environment, their participation in further problem-solving and program development feeds greater opportunity in the higher level motivational factors.

ORGANIZATIONAL CULTURE

As employees and managers gain cultural awareness and a global perspective through the process of virtualization in the organization, the culture of the organization will shift to one of global awareness. An often found side effect of globalization is the added bonus of becoming a learning organization, open to new experiences, and drawing employees and managers closer together in sharing relationships. Openness and acceptance to the differences each employee offers to the organization brings about new levels of sharing, and an environment which allows for greater self-disclosure, forming a culture in which safety, trust, and a team identity may form.

This often happens as managers and employees must learn to lean upon each other for their experiences with other cultures. In my work group alone we have employees that have recently arrived from India, Pakistan, France, Russia, Germany, Ireland, and England, to name only a few of the represented cultures. In addition to these nations, corporate travels have included additional trips to Argentina, Mexico, Romania, Taiwan, Singapore, as well as several Nordic nations as we reach out for greater awareness and understanding of the cultures with whom we work. In order to accomplish this, our organization must work with employees and managers alike to ensure a good understanding of the cultures in order to bring about strong working relationships.

As the corporate culture grows to that of a global family, social awareness and identification with the company and team may grow, strengthening a perception of equitable application of corporate and work group policy (Lipponen et al., 2004). This may then in turn strengthen one's pride in self and team, potentially increasing a sense of safety and acceptance and producing the necessary environment to allow vulnerability for establishment of trust. As Elving and Halgin have described for us, a sense of family will bring to the organization an expectation for an enduring relationship and a heightened sense of belonging and commitment (2005; 2009).

We all realize that not every corporation or company can realistically move employees around the globe as a means of engendering cultural awareness and the growth of familiarity. We can, however, take advantage of available technology in video conferencing. This technology is often available for a minimal monthly cost, and an inexpensive laptop.

TRAINING AND DEVELOPMENT

Job sharing for key individuals in key positions as a way building a strong understanding of the company, of the many corporate and individual cultures represented in each of these groups, and of the roles and goals of dependent organizations is a solid and proven means of building relationships among groups and teams. As employees and managers shift roles in a job rotation or job sharing process within the organization they will strengthen the effect of information sharing building relationships, and furthering a global perspective of the organization. In addition, the need for fast and effective learning and a newly contrived dependency upon new peers and employees, may bring with it an opportunity for peer training and mentoring, and a greater extension of openness and trust not previously available to virtual work teams. As Abernethy, Piegari, and Reichgelt (2007) note, the experience of mentored, guided training, lends itself well to virtual work teams as the trainer is able to adjust to the needs of the trainee based on feedback, and therefore better assess the degree to which the training fulfills the goals of the organization.

Peer training in a job rotation program also has the effect of providing employees with greater skill and understanding of the full life cycle of the product, providing for growth, greater commitment, and self-direction and motivation as the employee is able to take part in the whole of the work (Herzberg, 1965). The need for internal initiative and commitment by the individual may bring about greater opportunity for leadership activities in employees as they engage in global work teams. As employees work in an environment that may require greater isolation from the core team, autonomy, situational and organizational awareness, and leadership skills are essential.

STANDARDIZED POLICY AND PROCEDURES

Standardized policies and procedures provide greater ability to bring employees together, and empower them toward decision-making and self-direction (Duarte and Snyder, 2006). Policies and procedures need to be documented in a format that provides for the flexibility to tailor actionable instructions for each project and individual team goals to support rapid and consistent team formation. This will help in establishing the capability to position teams within the greater organization for successful goal attainment (Duarte and Snyder, 2006).

As the organization comes together with a set of standard practices, and team members across the organization learn that they can work in similar ways toward dependent goals, building a set of standard work templates will help in building program stability. Standardization of the templates with which teams document project information in application and product development further creates the ability to bring together team members, providing for rapid team normalization, and greater ability to support the high level of activity that virtual teams often must support.

Utilizing a standard set of policy statements and organizational procedures supports the rapid deployment of virtual teams, and allows for the use of a decentralized work teams as needed; however, maintaining balance between control of the process and the attempt to develop autonomy and trust is essential to corporate health (Gassman and von Zedtwitz, 2003; Gallivan, 2001). Standardization also supports institutional equity as the need for virtual teams to characterize and rationalize fairness and equity in practices may be reduced as standardization increases. Corporations must maintain the identity of the organization in order to be able to fully support the needs of globally participating teams.

LEADERSHIP SUPPORT OF VIRTUAL TEAMS

Behaviors such as team coordination and planning, clear definition and separation of responsibility, and autonomy of activity, are effective in preventing overlap, and need to be provided by team leadership. Leadership should also find ways to promote and support a consistent and continuous way to maintain active coordination of socialization activities to provide adequate levels of face-to-face participation (Moore, 2007; Sternberg and Grigorenko, 1993). Managers also need to find ways in which to ensure that team members have the specific technology they need that is tailored to the needs of their project wherever possible, and the capability to effectively implement the technology provided to them for collaboration (Duarte and Snyder, 2006; May and Carter, 2000).

Additionally, technology must be effectively integrated such that different technologies are compatible for information sharing, and integrated with that of the greater corporation to support communications (Duarte and Snyder, 2006; May and Carter, 2000). While this seems like a simple statement, we have seen in large organizations times where decentralized control has allowed too much independence in the area of technology choice. Such decisions as which web-based meeting software to use need to be centralized to prevent different groups from making independent decisions that may limit collaboration. At the same time, these decisions need to be integrated with other technology decisions to ensure the tools that are chosen will operate correctly with regionally determined applications.

TEAM LEADER AND TEAM MEMBER COMPETENCY DEVELOPMENT

Moore (2007) suggests that leadership competency regarding establishment of clear, concise, and achievable goals is essential to the success of virtual teams. Active engagement with the team members to provide timely feedback and effective guidance is necessary to identify roadblocks and prevent conflict, as well as supporting team members to come together to resolve discrepancies and maintain forward motion in the face of blocking issues and other unforeseeable challenges. Team members and management alike must be capable of building relationships across cultural and organizational verticals, and geographic boundaries (Duarte and Snyder, 2006). Skills in project management, relationship networking, electronic communication mediation tools, and personal boundary awareness are essential skills for virtual team members to develop and establish as norms within the virtual setting (Duarte and Snyder, 2006).

TEAM COLLABORATION MEDIATION

Andres (2002) suggests that studies consistently reflect the need for electronic mediation in communications as a team building tool in order that decision-making may be consistently distributed throughout the team to support team member participation. Teams such as those engaged in collaborative activities requiring high levels of participative mediation to support project processes may require media rich technology such as video conferencing.

In a recent study researchers noted that trust, either personality based, institutionally based, or cognitively based, are all positively influenced by the use of video conference technology. Teams that were found to be inconsistent in the use of video conference technology, however, were found to have varying degrees of success in improving team member trust that seemed to correlate with the degree of trusting behavior. Younger team members' awareness of team member needs, and their identification with the team, may not be as positively correlated to the high frequency of video conference use as are the older team members (Karpiscak, 2007).

Chat rooms, asynchronous blogging and feedback, posting and pulling information from peers, and peer to peer pressure and mentoring of participation in community to share knowledge are active and passive ways in which peer relationships may contribute to knowledge distribution and employee engagement in peer mentoring (Ardichvili, et al., 2003; Hale, 2000; Liu and Batt, 2010). The integration of the electronic work space according to May and Carter must incorporate all of the electronic enablers into one system of communication and information sharing (2000).

To summarize this chapter, Management governance provides the path upon which the teams travel. In addition to a good level of governance hygiene, it is critical to shift management focus from process compliance to process behavior. The transformation success rates can be greatly influenced by assessing the organization's readiness and identifying the right projects for the selected methods. Reinforcing new behaviors is essential to making the shift from a traditional life cycle, and prerequisite in the process of maturing in the new methods and organizational norms.

Chapter 6
Organizational Institutionalization

Now we are getting back to the basics. It doesn't really matter what kind of change we are talking about. Change can be good or bad, but very likely the work of change is agnostic when it comes to comparisons of goodness. Agile and lean is one such change that is really never measured by degrees of goodness by the employees, but rather measured by degrees of completeness. So often employees are led down the merry path of agile righteousness. As the agile and lean evangelists move through the organization everyone is appraised of the degrees of agile and the regaled with the weightlessness of lean as they plan their soiree, moving down the halls of marble arm in arm toward the bright lights at the end of the implementation and regaled with the waiting riches of agile project success.

As the party dies down and the lights are raised to signal to all the evening has ended, the credits roll, and the band begins to play their last song of the evening, and reality sets in we look around to find the streets aren't paved in gold and the treasure chest is likely only half filled. In other words, the reality we find at the end of the implementation may not be all that it was cracked up to be. Why? The answer is not necessarily in the implementation process if in fact we did the work up front to bring about a culture capable of support agile and lean methods. The problem may actually lie in the follow up process. Change management 101 course practitioners will tell, whenever anyone is willing to listen, that change, if not supported with effective methods of institutionalization will, at first glimpse of hard times, revert. People will almost in every case go back to what made them successful in the past when the present gets tough if the change is not fully institutionalized.

Institutionalized means to make the change a part of the way in which work gets done, or the way in which members of the institution are expected to behave or operate. It means to make the change a part of the culture and process of the organization. This step is often lost in the implementation because it requires follow through. When the change makes it into the "get the work done" stage, the follow up fails to happen, and we do believe this is due to people having moved on to other work. The Four Spheres Model of Agile and Lean Transformation model accounts for the need to follow the process through to the end when institutionalizing change in order to make agile and lean methods of getting work done stick.

Making change stick requires four main actions in the Organization Institutionalization Sphere.

- Facilitation.

- Reinforcement.

- Assessment.

- Enablement.

Facilitation, reinforcement, assessment, and leadership are essential elements in every institutionalization phase. Facilitation of change is essential to ensure the team remains focused on the goals and employs the right methods and tools. Reinforcement provides the glue that ensures the changes are valued, and the right behaviors are rewarded, while effective assessment gives assurance that the end goals are in sight and the proper trajectory maintained throughout the change process. Finally, the leaders of the organization will require measures and metrics that display for them a true picture of the state of change and the projected end goals in a way that is both relevant and meaningful to them, thus giving them the insight to focus on what they can do to ensure the desired outcome.

Change Requires Facilitation

Change, in order to create small group membership, needs to be facilitated. What this means is to have a professional, someone that works to instill the ability within the group to talk openly, share among the group the knowledge and experiences of the members in order that the conversation is on target and on topic. Keeping the conversation flowing is essential to instill the concept of small group membership that can then transition to a team environment. In this case, conflict may be good as it helps to clear the air, open the conversation in new areas that may, in later months, derail the changes as people go back to rehash topics in which they chose to agree to disagree rather than come to consensus, ensuring the groups are facilitated until they become a team with strong membership.

At times, having a seat at the table, rather than a transient membership that comes with random seating, can have the effect of committing an individual to the group rather than that person's identification remaining with the larger department. What this means is the person's self-identification remains as part of a larger organization rather than with the smaller group. We can see this happen in meetings as when the group comes together on a weekly basis and each person with regular attendance stakes out their normal place in the meeting by sitting in the same seat every time. Other team members will point this out to anyone that comes to the meeting for the first time and sits in "Charlie's chair." That chair normally occupied by Charlie, while not permanently assigned to Charlie is not open for anyone else to sit in without causing a disruption to the team.

These group assignments regarding one's normal place in the room is important to both the group, and to "Charlie's place on the team." Trained group facilitators know this and can use these membership tools to the advantage of the group to shape the group into a team. Having a place at the table, as opposed to sitting at any available seat as Millward, Haslam and Postmes (2007) point out, causes the group member to identify themselves more closely to the team than to the overall organization, and gives the group member a sense of membership. In this way the sense of team identify can overpower the sense of corporate identify and bring the group together as a team, thus opening up the conversation.

Creating membership in the place of corporate identity can be accomplished even when the team is first forming and help to establish the identity where one may not readily form, and can be facilitated in a virtual format as well. Creating a cadence and similarity in the way in which the group comes together may simulate the common seating phenomenon, and move the group to membership that then facilitates the conversation and a shift in thinking. It is the simple things such as seating, or the simulation of a common seating environment that can quickly establish that home feeling that can solidify changes that we need to use as a tool to institutionalize new ways within an organizational setting.

A great example of the hard work being done in the right ways, and yet the changes were never institutionalized. Over the past three years a wonderful major telecommunications firm made the decision to fundamentally change the way their quality program functions. The company spent the money by committing a team of quality professionals to complete an in depth self-evaluation of every aspect of the way they get work done. The team detailed a model of the quality department in their future; a factory model test organization. IT factories are a popular way of describing the use of fungible resources, or persons with the technical depth and breadth to move from project to project across the internal disciplines of the organization. Factories require a baseline set of skills and processes that may be used across all project disciplines to ensure that, no matter the project, team members across the projects know how work gets done.

In the factory model, the process remains the same while the technology may change with the project. The self-assessment team created the questions and the analysis model, identified specific gaps using the assessment analysis, and established cross-organizational working teams from the department IT engineers to close the gaps by creating a baseline set of processes and. Procedures. Each of the teams was mentored through the analysis and process development to ensure they used effective analysis and process design methods. Teams presented their projects to a governance board of directors at pre-established milestones to be sure the organizational leadership were in tune with their proposed changes, and all the teams presented their changes to their peers and managers prior to the implementation stage. Each one of the new processes was tried out by piloting the change on a representative "live" project to ensure the change worked and would be acceptable to a wider audience, made their "tweaks" to the process and any templates, and finalized their process change.

As the teams neared completion of the new processes they prepared training modules and delivered training in a "lunch and learn" format providing food and beverage in an informal setting to help bring in the students and ensure they enjoyed the training experience. When the training was complete a final meeting was held to ensure the directors were once again brought into the discussion to ensure they were fully aware of the remaining steps in the process. A small team of quality assurance people were enlisted to check and be sure the new process templates were used on every project that was deemed appropriate for use. This team, it was decided by the department vice president, would be an offshore contingent from our strategic partners to limit the cost. Their first role was to establish a quality management system folder to maintain the new process documents and templates and design a system that would ensure the project teams would be able to comply with the new processes with very little effort.

Making this happen, the team determined, would be simplest if the quality assurance team developed a means by which, whenever a project was kicked off part of the kick off was for the quality assurance team to identify the needed templates, create a work folder on the quality management system (QMS) site, and populate the site with the necessary templates and a tracking template that would automatically log the dates each document was changed, thus automating the most basic compliance check. The QMS site also included automated reports for each manager documenting the percent of compliance to the new process based on the automated-check for updates. As a final step, each week the reports were shared with the directors at the weekly director meeting to be sure the directors had the report and knew how well their teams comply with the changes.

By now we are sure you are waving your flag and thrilled with the way this project worked out. A great success by any measure. Right? By the end of the first 90 days the reports were green across the board showing 100 percent compliance for the department. Yet, the project essentially failed. Compliance, when the quality assurance team looked beneath the numbers, was terrible.

What happened was not in the planning, the change analysis, or the implementation process, but rather the leaders lacked the endurance for the long haul. The problem didn't really exist in the quality assurance check either, although it was somewhat inadequate as it only checked to ensure the documents were in the folder and a change had been made to the template. In reality the problem was with the leadership. In the end, the team members on the projects discovered, or perhaps maybe only began to sense, that the leaders to whom they reported did not have the endurance for the long haul. They lacked the fortitude to carry the process through the hard times, and so compliance began to wane. Compliance soon came to mean that the template updates were no longer meaningful, and when team members realized that simply changing the date was flagged as compliant, then the date change was the only step toward compliance.

Now the quality assurance team began to note the degradation in the lack of true compliance in their reports, but the reaction from the directors was less than enthusiastic. They, of course, would take a note and promise follow up with their teams, but in the end the drive and follow through needed to ensure their employees were convinced that they cared was not enough. After several more months of lack-luster reinforcement compliance for the new processes that would baseline the work practice in preparation for the factory model dropped to zero. This happens in a lot of cases and may be due to the theory that bosses like people who behave like they behave.

Recent studies have shown that bosses tend to like and promote people that dress like they dress and behave like they behave (Carter, 2013). People pick up on what others like and dislike very quickly. We all like to be liked and we all like to get accolades and promotions at work. Being a part of the team and accepted as a member is of extreme importance in an agile world, and very much just as important in the change process. This means that in the institutionalization phases, when the project team is working to be sure that the agile behaviors that the leaders desire become a valued part of the way in which work gets done, leaders must also reflect those behaviors. Reinforcing desired behaviors is a team effort and an essential element of the Four Spheres Model of Agile and Lean Transformation.

Desired Behaviors Must Be Reinforced

Leaders need to reinforce the desired behaviors in the way that they act every day, in their daily speech, and in the behaviors they both reinforce and extinguish through their own example. This means that the quality assurance review of the process must be more than a cursory review that something happened as in our example above, and check that the behaviors necessary to work in an agile process are the behaviors that occur. In our previous example the desired behavior was the execution of a common process that includes common work templates and not the population of the work folder. The work folder of which the quality assurance team used to provide a common store location for the templates was only incidental in making the access of the templates easy for the project team, and not the desired behavior. In this case, the process of reinforcement broke down when the directors expressed, through their own behavior, their acceptance of only cursory compliance.

A greater question then becomes, how does a leader extinguish poor behavior? In the past, and likely the way in which most of us were trained as parents, the prevailing wisdom was to ignore bad behavior in order to prevent accidently reinforcing the bad behaviors with the desired response. Most of us as parents have experienced, or at least witnessed, for those readers who were blessed with the well-behaved child, the expertly executed temper tantrum in the grocery store aisle. This scene always includes an exhausted and humiliated parent as they attempt to ignore the child's wailing as it echoes off the cinder block walls and tiled floors and equally irritated shoppers that glower, knowing they too have had or will soon have their own turn. These same parents with the wailing child will soon rise up to be the next generation of senior leaders with the responsibility of extinguishing the poor behaviors in the work place and will, as the leaders in our example, likely choose to ignore the poor behaviors in the work place.

Now some readers may choose to argue. You may actually be shouting at the pages right about now demanding that good managers do not ignore poor behaviors. You may insist that poor workers are coached, trained, resupplied, reassigned, or removed from the organization, and hopefully, we will add here, in that particular order. The list of actions is correct, but only in the case of poor performance. We are not talking about a performance issue in this chapter, but rather a behavior issue. Good managers will always recognize a performance issue and take the necessary steps to change poor performance. After all, performance is the bottom line for every organization and the immediate purpose of leadership. We must keep in mind, however, that poor performance does not necessarily mean poor behavior.

Changing behaviors is just a little more complicated than changing performance. In the case of needing to change performance, the desired outcome is very clear-cut in most cases. Performance levels are normally well defined and easily tracked based on predefined indicators, and one set of metrics may be tracked against peers and past or future metrics reports. Behaviors, on the other hand, are not as easily measured and often are not clearly defined, and almost never measured. It should also noted that when we are discussing poor behaviors in the this context we are not necessarily talking about poor behaviors in the sense that one may act out when angry, but rather behaviors that do not line up well with the newly desired behaviors of a lean or agile organization.

Agile and lean behaviors include open and continuous communication using all of the available channels. Remember that communication is a two-way process. It must include listening as well as transmitting with both of the skills focused on the clarity of the message. Team members must have agreement on how decisions are attained, and be able to disagree and work through the disagreement, come to a decision and keep moving. They make their own schedules and plan their own work. They make commitments to their team members based on their plan and keep those commitments. As a team, they hold one another to those commitments knowing that the commitments give their department the ability to make commitments to the leadership and the larger population of stakeholders.

This raises the question, what does poor behavior look like in an agile setting? Felps, Mitchell, and Byington (2006) conducted a study to determine if the behavior of one *Bad Apple* really can have a detrimental effect on an agile team's capability. Since agile is a contact sport, to use a common American euphemism, one's ability to play well in groups is of extreme importance, thus poor behaviors as outlined by Felps et al. include withholding one's effort from the group, expressing negative effect, and violating those norms defined by and held dear by the group. Each of these behaviors has an effect upon the team relationships that may include a reduction in trust and therefore a limit on the team's flexibility and ability to take on risk.

Almost every team has experienced the team member that withholds effort. We often experience this behavior beginning in adolescence and continuing through college and in to the work place. This happens regardless of the type of work we do, but can be devastating in a team environment where the work output tends to be in the form of knowledge. Taking the free ride, or loafing as Felps et al. name the behavior, has the effect of producing the feeling of inequity. For an agile team, the effect can be debilitating. If you can remember back to your days in college or perhaps even a more recent feeling that things just are not fair in your work place. These feelings can sneak in due to different events such as at raise or bonus time, or when a co-worker is promoted, and yet no one can come up with a good reason why "so-and-so" was treated so much better than the rest of the team.

Don't forget that feelings matter. In the end, when inequity is real or just perceived, feelings can lead to a reduction in institutional trust. Team members will soon believe that not everyone is treated equally. They may believe in favorites among team members or that some teams working the coveted, high profile jobs will benefit from their positions with greater pay and job advancement opportunities simply due to their role rather than their skill. As the team's suspicion of inequity grows, and the ill feelings are shared among team members and perhaps even across teams, team members will begin to seek more evidence. They begin to look for reinforcement of their belief and perhaps begin to dig about for information perhaps leading to a false reinforcement. As their ill feelings take hold and more information comes to light the poor behavior may begin to erode relationships within the team causing individual members to choose act out and withdraw their emotional support for the team. They may choose to not trust other team members as they take a hit in the area of Cognitive Trust as they begin to take on the characteristics of the bad apple (Dando, 2013).

Negativity on the team is every bit as destructive a behavior as shirking one's responsibilities. Remember meeting that person at work that just drags down your day. When approached with a smile and a delightful "Good morning to you" they will always respond with a ready retort of "What's so good about it?" If you are like most you will quickly respond, "I'm alive," as you try to salvage your good feelings and bright outlook and quickly move toward any bright light in the room. Bad vibes is an oft used euphemism for negativity. Negative people give off an aura of bad feelings everywhere they go. They sap the energy and zap the synergy, drawing off team members focus toward defending their good mood, schedule, and work load to ensure the team is able to meet deadlines and quality projections.

Negativity, according to Felps et al., is asymmetric in the way it affects or changes team dynamics. Not all members are susceptible to the cancer that is negativity, and not all members will react or cope in the same way. Negativity moves through a team like a cancer, chewing its way slowly from member to member, reducing outputs as members become less gruntled with both their work and the institution, and perhaps their place in the team. Camacho and Paulus (1995) conducted a study that determined that negativity does indeed significantly reduce the creative output of a team. They went on to note, and their study does agree with Felps et al., that negativity in the team may reduce the creativity of a team to the level equal to a team that is entirely negative. When we look closely at these studies it becomes apparent that negative behaviors on a team may reduce the creative outputs of the team by almost 40 percent. It seems in this case that the negative person on the team is perhaps not performing as a team member, and may have the same effect on the team as perhaps an absent member.

Participation and supporting the emotional and skill needs of the team are an important part of membership as is upholding those things that a team holds dear to itself. These norms are the team's identity, the way they do what they do. Violating team norms is taboo. It's like badmouthing the team mascot or rejecting the team colors for those colors more in tune with your personal taste. Violating team norms is just not done. Withholding one's efforts from the team and spreading negativity are simply specific topics of violation as are norms of expected interpersonal behaviors. Team membership functions much like family membership. Members must make the effort and perform the necessary work to make the relationship function properly (Halgin, 2009). As with home and other familial relationships, members have the responsibility to regulate their expressions of feelings to appropriate opportunities of expression to ensure their personal feelings are not disruptive or harmful to the greater good of the team.

In the institutionalization of agile and lean methods, both of which are team-based behavioral focused methods, the leadership of the organization must ensure that the teams are prepared and able to handle the bad behaviors from within the team. Dando offers three potential reactions to the bad apple (2013). Accept the bad behavior and do the best you can as a team, plan ahead with predetermined acceptable behaviors and remedies, or eliminate the bad apples by removing them from the team before they can infect the rest of the team members. Whichever method of coping that the team chooses, the leadership should stand ready to help the team to be successful.

Leadership responsibility must not be discounted. Remember that the leadership responsibility in an agile or lean environment is to ensure that obstacles to success are removed. This is the key to effective institutionalization of agile and lean methods within any organization, for when problems and difficulties arise, if the proper behaviors are not positively reinforced and most importantly enabled, people will always revert to the behaviors that had made them successful in the past. This includes removing any opportunity for the placement of blame when problems do happen. Leaders need to ensure that everyone understands that the leaders do not want to hear who is to blame, but rather they are interested in ensuring the root of the problem is identified and eliminated. In the case of bad behavior this means that the leaders need to support the agile and lean teams in whatever way they choose to act upon the bad behaviors up to and including the removal of the bad actor if the team deems removal necessary.

Getting back to reinforcement of the desired behaviors. Reinforcement then requires the ability of the leadership team to catch people doing good. To accomplish this the reporting and measurement program needs to be realigned to match the agile and lean behaviors to provide the leaders the ability to identify and capture good, and the drive out bad behavior. The tracking should be able to measure the cadence of the daily standups and the forward progress, or velocity, of the team. Both of the measures will help the leadership to determine how well the team is setting pace and their ability to sustain their forward momentum. Another great measure is that of customer satisfaction and in particular the customers' measure and perception of quality in the products provided. In both lean and agile team environments, it is this measure that counts the most.

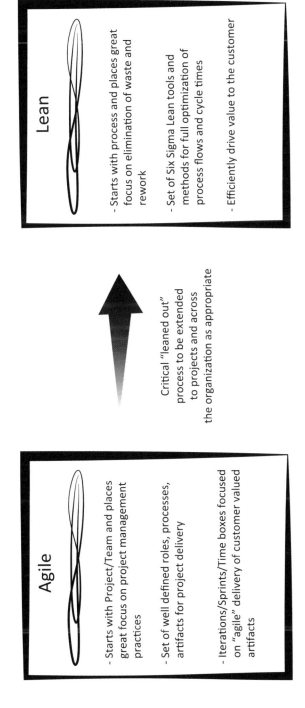

Agile

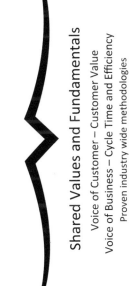

- Starts with Project/Team and places great focus on project management practices

- Set of well defined roles, processes, artifacts for project delivery

- Iterations/Sprints/Time boxes focused on "agile" delivery of customer valued artifacts

Critical "leaned out" process to be extended to projects and across the organization as appropriate

Lean

- Starts with process and places great focus on elimination of waste and rework

- Set of Six Sigma Lean tools and methods for full optimization of process flows and cycle times

- Efficiently drive value to the customer

Shared Values and Fundamentals

Voice of Customer – Customer Value
Voice of Business – Cycle Time and Efficiency
Proven industry wide methodologies

Figure 6.1   **Lean and agile are complimentary**

But how do we drive an organization in the direction of lean and agile methods and ensure that the changes such as described above are fully integrated into the way work gets done. We call this institutionalized. Change must take into account both the human needs and the methodologies involved. It requires a thorough articulation of the current state and the desired state in a way that will facilitate a description of the gap between the two. We believe one of the best ways of finding this gap, and one that maintains the focus on the behaviors necessary to institutionalize agile and lean within the organization is to choose an assessment that focuses on the behaviors of agile and lean teams.

Making change happen in the way that organizations get work done requires a continuous process of checking and adjustment, and so the final element in the Organizational Institutionalization sphere of the Four Spheres Model of Agile and Lean Transformation is the regularly schedule reassessment. Lean and agile methods share a lot of characteristics that allow for a behavioral based assessment. Both have well defined processes and measures and a focus on the customer, and both require well defined roles and responsibilities with a desire to eliminate the waste in the product life cycle (see Figure 6.1 on the previous page).

Planning the Assessment

As the champions of the change prepare for a current state assessment they need to begin the process, in this particular case, with the future state in mind. Every assessment process should be able to answer the management dilemma, and for these managers the dilemma may be described as something like this. This is the dilemma we used recently at a nationally recognized telecommunications company:

> *My organization has made a decision to use agile and lean methods in order to improve the ability to better satisfy customer desires for new and effective products and to fulfill the customer defined expectations of quality. How do we know if the department is able to support the use of agile and lean methods? (Anonymous, n.d.)*

We chose this dilemma because it allowed the freedom to express several management questions that need to be answered to fully describe a resolution to the dilemma. Our quest began with the expression of a few management questions.

- Are we currently operating in agile ways?

- Are we currently operating in lean ways?

- What are the high level categories of lean behaviors relevant to our engineering life cycle?

- What are the high level categories of agile behaviors relevant to our engineering life cycle?

- What are the behaviors normally found in an agile life cycle that we need to encourage?

- What are the behaviors normally found in a lean life cycle that we need to encourage?

In order to provide answers to the management questions, we established some research questions by which we were able to create a basic set of survey questions. The research questions were established in both lean and agile surveys and off we went to do great things.

The lean categories by which we focused our survey were restricted to the topics of process, metrics, training and tools (see Figure 6.2 on the next page). These categories were created in order to prevent expressing new categories to our respondents, and in this way not causing a questionnaire reader to build a new context around each of the survey questions. Categories such as in Figure 6.2 would normally be found within the standard Quality Management System, and should therefore provide a standard context as the respondent is reading the questions around what may be considered the behaviors we would expect to find in effective agile and lean teams.

As we prepared for the survey the research team chose to use the current project list from each of the test directors and thus covering the entire population of products and services that the department supported. Each of the project teams in the department was asked to provide two contacts, or proposed respondents. These respondents were then asked to provide the names of their engineering counterparts, both upstream and downstream from their position in the engineering life cycle to ensure the survey covered, at minimum their direct life cycle customers.

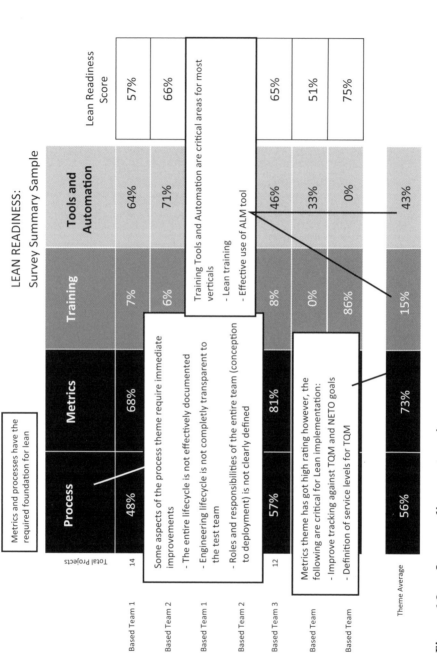

Figure 6.2   Lean readiness categories

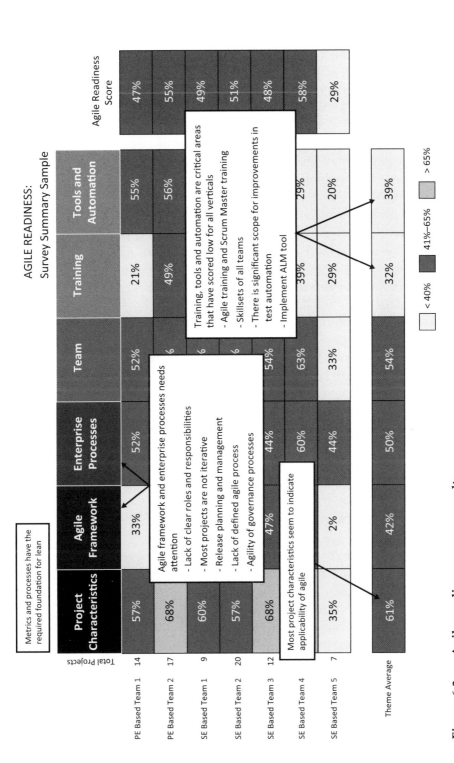

Figure 6.3 Agile readiness survey results

By including this minimum set of respondents the survey analysis would also provide the ability to determine whether the organizations that would be working together on agile or lean projects were at the same level of capability to support the new project paradigm. Each respondent to the lean survey was asked to provide an answer to 28 questions divided up as 13 process questions, 11 metrics questions, 1 in tools and automation, and 3 in training. Each one of the questions was based on the expected behaviors that a lean practitioner would expect to portray when performing specific functions. The questions for agile methods followed much the same pattern. In each of the categories, the questions provided the ability to determine which projects were following the agile method framework and whether or not the project teams upstream and downstream partners were in the same point of the capability development process. This survey used eight project characteristics questions, twelve in the agile framework category, nine for enterprise processes, six for tools and automation, and four each for the training and team categories.

As was the output for the lean behavior assessment, as shown in Figure 6.3 on the previous page, the agile assessment portion of the survey created a heat map by which the directors for each product test area and their upstream and downstream partners were able to visually identify areas of strength and weakness. Where strengths were found, the leaders of the department were able to spread these good practices and opportunity to share experience across the teams to provide a catalyst for organizational learning. Points of weakness were immediately apparent based on the light grey shading, as shown in Figure 6.3.

Give Your Leaders the Opportunity to Care

What the survey results provided was the ability for leaders to care about the transition process and a guide that allowed them to take specific actions to reinforce their expectations. Institutionalization of organizational change is about making sure the desired behaviors have positive reinforcement, but to accomplish reinforcement of the new behaviors requires the ability to discover areas of good behavior as well as finding the pockets of not so good behavior in order to reinforce the change with training and coaching opportunity.

Positive reinforcement of desired behaviors makes the team member feel good about making the change. As Joseph (2014) pointed out in a recent online article, giving positive feedback to team members that step out and take a chance on being strong and positive members of the new way things get done club helps by eliminating the fear and self-doubt that come with changing the way one behaves. It adds to the team member's self-worth, and increases the probability that the behavior will be repeated in the future and the likelihood that other team members will be willing to act in the same way. Perhaps of even greater importance to the leadership is the idea that the team member who received the positive reinforcement may be more likely to reach out to other employees and help them to make the transition to the new way of acting as well.

Along these same lines, if in fact the leaders have chosen agile and lean methods as the way work gets done, then when teams or employees do not behave the way the leadership desires, then leaders need to be prepared to withhold praise. This means that when a project is successful in spite of the team members not having behaved according to the leaders desired new way of getting work done, the leaders must be prepared to not provide the usual positive reinforcement. This will immediately get the point across that how work gets done is every bit as important as getting the work done, and will tend to cause the team to behave more in line with the team and team members that are receiving praise.

Chapter 7

Lean Manufacturing: A Case in Study

MICHAEL P. WISE

In a time when the world has grown so small that our competition both knows us well and at times is us, leaders must keep their ears to the ground, listening for every little nuance and change in the tools available to stay combat ready. How can we be our own competition? You might want to know why us. Combat ready? Oh, those in executive leadership will recognize the analogy, as they are the ones leading the risk analysis, checking the intelligence reports and realigning resources and priorities to head off the next attack across the global landscape. Lean is a tool which, while not new to the tool bag, is enjoying a resurgence as Western organizations take notice of the operational efficiencies enjoyed by practitioners.

Senior leaders understand the urgency and necessity of cutting the cost of utilities and operating costs in raw materials and electrical usage, and eliminating waste such as packaging material used for delivery of parts. They even understand the need to eliminate the kinds of waste we find in raw materials lost during the manufacturing process due to inefficient processing or positioning of equipment, and the need to improve the operational efficiency of each piece of equipment and the processes used in the manufacturing through old school practices such as time-motion reduction and checklists to reduce transition times. With this introduction to lean it is important to realize that lean manufacturers look at lean a bit different than lean thought workers. In thought industry such as engineering and information technology lean is a way of thinking about ones work. Reductions in waste are often seen as a reduction in the work that gets done. Less documentation and fewer heavy functions or calls can make a product lean. Eliminating risk or even an increase in quality assurance early in the product life cycle can be said to be lean. Lean manufacturing is a bit different in the nature of the work.

Lean Manufacturing is loosely defined by researchers as a socio-technical system whose main objective is to eliminate waste by reducing supplier, customer, and internal variability (Hasle, Bojesen, Jensen, and Bramming, 2012). Variability, to give a two second lesson in process management, is the natural or inherent differentiation in processing that is in all processes. This may mean, for example, that if my process requires the drilling of a 0.250 access hole in the door hinge for mounting a door to a steel locker, then the actual measure of the hole may naturally vary between the measures of 0.246 and 0.259. The differences in the measure may account for the wobble in the drill, the positioning of the piece in the press, differences in the rotation of the drill motor, or perhaps even the rate at which the drill wears down. Every process in manufacturing and for that matter writing software code has within that process an amount of natural variation. Variability, therefore, is found within the processing accomplished by suppliers, customers, and internal processing departments and will be found, not perhaps be found, but will be found in every process from purchasing to manufacturing, to logistics and shipping.

The Four Spheres Model: Individual Behaviors

Researchers use the term socio-technical system because this definition identifies the need for change by employees in how they perform their job and how they relate to the organization, as well as how leadership will change the work procedures, workflow, life cycle, and overall structure and organization of the departments, divisions, and workflow. A great amount of the work in lean takes place in the first of the Four Spheres Model as employees are asked to make a transition from a position of compliance with procedures and following direction established by the leaders of the organization to being a part of the decision-making. Leaders will begin to ask employees for their input and request that they use critical thinking strategies to continually improve their work processes. Just following orders and complying with the way work gets done is no longer enough.

The transition to taking responsibility for the way work gets done is never easy. Employees are asked to grow in the hierarchy of group development from dependence upon leaders for decisions and guidance such as job assignments or perhaps even job stops, to accepting responsibility where none existed in the past. Accepting more responsibility is difficult for employees that are accustomed to following directions and having a routine each day, not making the decisions and driving the daily direction of the organization.

The Four Spheres Model: Team Roles and Responsibility

Their new responsibilities are somewhat reverse from what the employees are used to and consider normal, and in some cases may be in conflict with traditional job roles or even group bargaining agreements. Employees are not only requested to start making essential engineering and manufacturing decisions, but are expected to make day-to-day decisions at the plant level, which affect the efficiency of the manufacturing process. They are now expected to drive innovation and to take the lead in building a company that is not only competitive in the industry but captures a leading position.

Does this sound like a big order for employees that until perhaps even yesterday were asked to put their chin down and get to work? Continuous improvement of organizational process and procedures is a role normally and traditionally reserved to well educated, higher level consultants and yet we are saying that even the person following a broom has the ability to contribute in making the company a lean fighting machine. The manager takes more of a coaching position or consultant role and assists the employees to take charge, accept responsibility and get comfortable in the drivers' seat of the facility. Organizational Development as a science will tell you that not all employees will be able to make the emotional and tactical changes necessary to thrive in the new environment. Some employees will leave and others may need to be reassigned or perhaps asked to leave.

BE PREPARED TO MAKE HARD CHOICES

Employees that remain with the company after the implementation of lean must be willing to accept their new role and responsibility. Their role now includes reducing variation in processes such as the suppliers' delivery of material and parts, customers' frequently changing order forecast and order placements, and the variability within their own organization such as changing production schedules and improvement plans. Implementing such tools as lean requires change, and change requires effective change management, and with effective change management comes the management responsibility to ensure the remaining employees have the support in knowledge and leadership necessary to make this all happen.

A great example of lean implementation and the struggles that come with that is my work with a global fortune 500 consumer goods manufacturing company with a strong history of success that has lasted for 90-plus years. This company produces chemical products, food products and specialty consumer products within a multitude of different industries and as with most successful companies the leaders were able to read the tea leaves and do their best to anticipate the future and begin making the needed changes. As margins in this industry became ever more thin and the pressures of the small world environment began to close around them, they chose to act rather than react. This ever-changing business environment and the expanding drive toward global business motivated the organizations' move toward implementing lean.

THE SENIOR LEADERS AT THIS PLACE OF EMPLOYMENT TOOK CHANGE MANAGEMENT TO HEART

They stepped up to ensure everyone had the vision. Following the advice of many a change management expert they talked and talked, and when they felt they had talked enough they talked some more to be sure everyone had the vision. With the implementation of lean manufacturing on the horizon, the corporate senior leaders traveled to all the manufacturing facilities in the United States to hold plant-wide meetings with the facility managers and hourly employees, detailing what was to come. They talked about their vision for the future and what it would mean to them. They talked about the commitment and the energy that this sort of work will demand and the fear of failure and the fear of the unknown that may come with the implementation. Naturally with this conversation came fear.

The Four Spheres Model: Management Governance

EVERYONE WILL GET NERVOUS

The level of nervous discussion made it clear that everyone, both employees and managers, was concerned for their future and their ability to fit in the new organization. When told about the lean initiative and the coming visit by the senior leaders of the organization fear and curiosity peaked, but at the same time they were a little excited to hear about the assumed improvements coming to the facility. In the manufacturing industry, improvement is a sign that the company sees a strong future for your site. Chatter was the outcome of nervous energy, and the days prior to the meeting were spent in endless water cooler discussions as everyone speculated on the content of their coming presentation.

The organization leaders used a power point, simple, direct, and concise, to express their expectations for employees during their on-site visit to highlight important information while introducing to the employees what lean is all about. They explained lean as both a way of thinking about work, and the need to highlight the needs of the customer as they go about their daily work. The leaders also explained that the implementation was to be accomplished in stages. The leaders recognized the concerns that the employees were experiencing and the need for them to absorb and acclimate to the changes that would be taking place and so wanted to limit the degree of change at any given time and so reduce the level of change they would experience.

The leaders introduced the different groups within the plant that would be developed to separate the future responsibility among the employees. They called these new groups pillars, or new behaviors and skills upon which the new organization will lean. While I will spend some time later in the chapter to fully describe these essential elements of the change, it was effective at the time to only express the names and roles within these pillars. The pillars identified by our corporate leaders for our company were Autonomous Maintenance, Safety, Production, Quality, and Logistics. Each pillar, or area of focus, would have a leader responsible creating new and solid processes to improve performance within their assigned area.

The Four Spheres Model: Organizational Institutionalization

EMPHASIS IS ON COMMITMENT

A major emphasis from the leaders was put on the level of commitment needed from each employee, not only for the success of the implementation, but also for the success of the employee after the implementation. Employees were told that they would need to take on additional daily responsibilities while increasing effort and performance in all they do, and anything short of total commitment would be considered a failure of their responsibilities. As the leaders expounded upon the extra work, it became clear that every employee was to become so much more than the traditional view of an employee in an American manufacturing environment. Employees were asked to step outside their comfortable daily routine and begin to take notice of the environment, or perhaps what many call their eco system. Leaders were asking that the employees take notice of the many people around them. They were asked to notice how the work of those upstream of their contribution, notice their peers in dependent functions and departments, and their internal and external customers that receive the output of their labors.

That additional responsibility described by the leaders consisted of responsibilities outside the normal requirements of the employees. These were responsibilities normally prescribed to their managers and perhaps ascribed to highly paid consultants in the past. They were asked to take part in additional daily decision-making opportunities and problem-solving activities. The reactions of the employees ranged from nervousness about the added responsibility and fears of failure to feeling upset at being asked to take on a role outside the job description to which they signed on when they came to this company. Others were excited. They felt this was a great way to have their voices heard and they welcomed the chance to contribute to the direction of the organization; however, while they became evangelists for change and eagerly sought out ways in which they could contribute and express their excitement, they were in the minority.

Working the Problem through All Four Spheres

PUT EVERYTHING ON THE TABLE

The senior leaders left nothing to interpretation during the meeting so all employees knew the added pressure ahead of them. In solid change management fashion they laid it all on the table in an attempt to fairly express their desire for change and make a full and clear disclosure regarding the future of their company and the vision to which they wanted all to ascribe. All employees understood that total commitment to a vision of lean manufacturing and personal responsibility for the quality and capability of the company was required. How committed they needed to be was driven home when they were asked at one point in the meeting to look at the person on their right, and then their left.

Amidst a mix of startled and somewhat amused grins, wide-eyed fear, and a few hesitant hellos from people who had not necessarily met in the past, almost everyone complied and made a quick glance from left to right. They were told to imagine a future in which, at some point in the near future, one of three people will not be with the company any more. The room fell silent as the executive explained further that, whether it be by attrition, employees leaving because they don't want to be part of this complicated process, or fired because they can't provide the level of commitment required by the leaders, but in any case the size of the organization would likely be shrinking. Change management 101 class room adjourned.

As leaders in organizational change and problem-solving, we realize that everyone must understand the threat, or at least that a threat exists. Everyone must be able to buy into the idea that there is a compelling need to be different is really made, and at this point it began to sink in. Lean wasn't just the new program of the month, but rather a new way of living for the company. Lean was their way of fending off the current competition and ensuring the company was positioned to take the lead as the dust settled in the industry. This statement made the employees fearful of what's coming and yet more attentive and ready to listen.

Even those who were excited about the chance to contribute at a higher level were nervous because of the overstated chance of failure. This statement, instead of motivating employees to step up and take charge of their future and the future of the organization, caused them to be more fearful and reluctant to step forward. The resource pool began to drain rather rapidly as many employees left feeling they were not able to make the commitment, or perhaps not capable of learning the new way of life. Some simply left the company because they thought the level of commitment was impossible to reach and that they would not have any opportunity to be successful to the level that the leaders said would be necessary. They felt leaving under their own power was the best choice to make at that time. Still others left because they were not willing to commit to the level described by the organizations leaders. The change and the commitment perhaps meant to them a need for self-study to come up to a knowledge level needed to thrive in the new lean environment that they were not willing to make. To others they felt their family life was more important than perhaps the extra college training they might need to catch up with the new training requirements. Others perhaps simply wanted to maintain their comfortable, uncommitted work life. Each was a valid decision for them to make in their own way and for their own interests. Either way, some good employees were lost and the others would need to pick up the slack and be prepared to help the new employees hired to replace those that left, while they themselves were trying to learn the new system. This added to the stress of this difficult time. In trying to motivate the employees and ensure they understood the magnitude of the endeavor they were undertaking, the leaders, whether intentionally or incidentally, forced out some employees who might have had a positive impact on the transition.

It seems, as I look back at that time, that perhaps a less heavy-handed introduction may have better served our management team. A combination of training, both on the job and classroom-based learning with a mix of specifically assigned computer-based learning, would have provided the insight and commitment needed. In addition to training, a certain level of stress reduction opportunities may have helped in allowing employees to express their fears openly and without the fear of being branded as uncommitted. Human resources support in establishing new job descriptions with employee input to support buy in, and perhaps even employee-developed subject matter expert delivered learning opportunities such as lunch and learns would have helped to bring along the less committed or change shy employees. Through these methods and others the vision of the company may have been delivered in ways that would make the employees, if not happy, at least more supportive in the short run up to change.

A CONSISTENT VISION AND A ROADMAP ARE NECESSARY

Most experts would agree that to have a successful lean implementation, a consistent vision and roadmap must be clearly communicated to all involved. The leaders within my organization successfully communicated the vision and roadmap, although in a way that seems to have instilled some fear and loathing. They provided a description and picture that the future employee's capabilities needed to have a successful lean implementation and successful career after the implementation. All employees fully understood the direction the organization was heading. However, by over-emphasizing the commitment, high rate of failure, and likelihood of personal failure and possible removal from the organization, the leaders scared the employees into leaving or being so afraid to fail that they could not sufficiently contribute to the implementation at a level of which they should have been capable. In their effort to create a sense of urgency, the leaders created an environment of fear that had the effect of freezing some employees in place, and chasing away others. The magnitude of the difficult change ahead of them certainly needed to be conveyed to all involved. This was part of the roadmap they were putting together for the lean implementation. The leaders wanted to be sure that everyone knew what was ahead, but in their zeal to convey an important message, they over-stressed the frightening part of the change.

There must be medium ground to emphasize the importance of commitment without creating an environment of fear. Communicating the level of commitment and pressure to implement lean is essential, but emphasizing the commitment while describing the vision and the roadmap will often be enough to motivate the employees to embrace the change while delivering the message of importance. Knowing the expectations is necessary to prepare, but with those expectations must come the comfort of knowing the organizational leaders are supporting both the initiative and the employees to ensure a successful implementation. With any organizational change, fear and anxiety should be removed to instil the trust in the organization needed by employees to endure and excel at the change ahead (Bhasin, 2012). It is this element of change management which the leaders of my organization not only failed to achieve, but they increased the fear and almost built an environment in which the employees felt they could not succeed.

Lean and agile methods are often considered dependent upon the ability of employees to feel that leaders have their backs as they learn the new ways. They need to feel they have the allowance of small failures as they come to grips with their new skills and responsibilities. As in every new endeavor, people have to take a risk as they step up to learn new skills and behaviors, and risk-taking requires the acceptance that failure is inevitable until the new skills become engrained in the way work gets done. Fear is the enemy of risk and the entrepreneurial behaviors that lean requires.

The meetings held by the senior leaders, while traumatic, were not a total loss. The successful communication of their vision was essential and effective in developing a shared meaning behind what lean means to their organization. Almost everyone was able to carry from the meeting a short stack of paper that provided a description of the end state with at least a high level organizational plan and some basic information regarding the changes to their work expectations. They now had the beginning of what was the description of what the organization would look like after the implementation. The leaders spent two hours in the meetings explaining the addition of pillars and pillar leaders. Pillars, in the way the leaders were using the term, were the divisions between areas of specific focus for the organization, and while the definitions of these areas will not change, how they may be specifically implemented within each group may vary between manufacturing locations. Pillars are the areas in which the company wants specific focus to be given, because they feel these areas are critical to organizational success. The pillars identified by our corporate leaders for our company were Autonomous Maintenance, Safety, Production, Quality, and Logistics. Each pillar, or area of focus, had a leader responsible for heading up this area and creating processes to improve performance within their area. The pillar leaders developed process flows with measures assigned at the entry and exit points and well as operational definitions for the measures and are charged with ensuring a focus on the customer as their pillar is matured.

Autonomous maintenance is a detailed preventive maintenance activity that typically includes the use of center-lining. Center-lining is a term used to describe the activity of marking the optimal operational settings for machine operations. This seems to be a process similar to what industrial mechanics would do when disassembling and reassembling machines to ensure the machine was put back together with parts such as couplings shell components in the same alignment as when they came apart. It is a process designed to simplify the set-up and realignment of components to ensure optimum operation and reduce the waste in rework and operational excess. Center-lining helps to make sure the equipment is aligned and within specification, and aids in identifying Kaizen events to in the important areas to during the maintenance work.

CENTER-LINING

Kaizen, like center-lining is a Six Sigma tool, and designed to be simple and easily integrated into the daily activities of machine engineers and operators without a large amount of statistical knowledge. Kaizen is based on the Japanese business philosophy of continuous process improvement rather than the event-driven improvement traditionally employed by American leaders. Ironically enough, we chose to employ a cross-breed we called Kaizen events, or activities that focus employee attention on a certain area of a piece of equipment. This attention involves an audit of the current state of the equipment, a preventive maintenance activity in which the normal parts are checked and replaced based on the number of hours the equipment has run, and a predictive activity which includes gauging and/or replacing parts based on a possible failure rate which is identified by maintenance logs on the equipment. Using this method successfully moved our maintenance efforts away from the normal process of run-to-failure, and into the realm of continuous process improvement capable of reducing the process variability caused by worn components and random down time. No longer would the line fail due to breakage that could have easily been predicted or prevented. Run times were now predictable and repeatable allowing for greater planning and just-in-time warehousing techniques which in turn leads to smaller inventory and less overtime.

Working in this way required both the line operators and the maintenance employees to accept the role of ownership on their equipment. They could no longer stand passively alongside their equipment and consider themselves successful in this role. Employees were becoming members of a greater team that required specific roles and responsibilities along with communication. Their new roles required relationships. Employees had to get to know one another and to communicate their findings and their concerns in order to make the new way of getting work done effective. Isolation, while once the acceptable norm, was now an antagonistic position.

The autonomous maintenance pillar attracted a lot of attention because of its focus on team-based performance increases and repeatability of equipment efficiency. Their success was a guiding beacon to the other pillars, and a motivational tool to bring other employees on board. Another successful pillar was that of safety. Led by a long-time employee with a diverse operational background and understanding of operations, maintenance and safety initiatives the safety pillar rapidly grew into an essential part of the company culture. The safety pillar leader worked closely with the Autonomous Maintenance lead to ensure safety procedures were followed. A key early area of focus was the improvements needed in the lockout-tag out program.

It would seem something as essential to the safety and well-being of employees would be an area that employees would have ensured was always up to standards, but this isn't always the case. I remember my years as an industrial mechanic quite clearly, and the hours spent in the hospital emergency room waiting to see the doctor due to making dumb decisions. Things that we thought were funny because we escaped serious injury like the acetylene gas balloons had to stop. Yes, it was funny to fill a plastic bag with explosive gas and watch it pop in a ball of flame. Sad, but true. Bigger things like cleanliness and orderliness had to be attended to in order to reduce the chance of injury and thus loss of both time and health. We took to heart the Five-S practice of Japanese manufacturing with implementation of the practice of sorting, setting in place, shining and sweeping, standardizing, and then sustaining the change. Taking risks can easily become part of the culture in the macho world of American industry. Shortcuts become the norm, and surprisingly can add many hours due to rework, damage to equipment, or injury and loss to the employees. People had to learn that risk, while at times is inherent in the work, must be carefully measured and managed. Safety standards were reviewed, reworked and updated to ensure they were up to the latest standards and then tracked to ensure they were properly utilized. The safety pillar is the only pillar which has a focus on the entire plant and all activities within the plant. All other pillars are focused in a certain department or area of the plant.

FIND AND MANAGE BEST PRACTICES

Production, quality and logistics pillars are self-explanatory to some degree. Implementation of best practices included documentation of the expected process and work instructions to ensure repeatability in these pillars as well.

We documented our metrics and operational methods and managed the practice with the use of metrics and reporting that enabled our ability to make fact-based decisions. The senior leaders did a great job of providing all the information needed for employees to fully understand the changes occurring within the company and how everyone would be affected. They provided regular reports that allowed employees to see how their work contributed to the overall health of the organization and how they performed in relation to their peers. Shift workers now had the ability to understand the work their peers on others shifts contributed to their own well-being. They could track the practices of their counterparts and call foul if they missed a checkpoint that could inevitably contribute to downtime or early ware in the equipment. One of the keys to lean operations is giving one's peers and managers the ability to care, and proper checklists and checkpoints is a simple method of making this happen.

After the senior leaders were finished with their meetings at the facilities, the plant leadership took over the responsibility to prepare the organization for sustainable change. The plant leadership team made up of the Plant Manager and all department heads met to develop a plant level plan to ensure the employees were prepared and that we could get the employees engaged and excited for the changes to come. Implementation plans were put in place, and a plant meeting was held to discuss the implementation as well as address the information passed from the organizations leaders. The level of commitment described by the leaders was addressed, and although the commitment was reinforced, it was toned down a little so as to not scare the employees into non-action. The employees were assured of receiving full backing from the plant leadership team and they were told that the managers would be working aside them to ensure a successful implementation.

WHAT THE EMPLOYEES NEEDED MOST WAS INFORMATION

They needed to understand how they fit within the new organization and how their skills were to grow and would be supported. It may sound cliché, but information is power and with shared information comes shared power and shared goals and relationships. As the employed grew in their awareness of the processes and goals within the new organization they were able to find their place and begin form trusting relationships with the new organization and their managers. The managers, it seems, were fearful as well, but had not disclosed this information with their peers or employees. As they came to learn of each other's needs and fears they were able to disclose to one another how they felt and how they coped with the new changes. This act of disclosure helped them each to find ways to support one another in learning their roles.

Each step of the implementation was communicated to the employees. One of the first steps in the implementation process was the identification of the Pillar owners. As the announcements were made the employees began to breathe more easily. The fog was lifting and teams were formed around the announced leaders. With the lifting of the shroud of secrecy employees were able to find their way and understand how they fit. The new owners with responsibility in building their new organizations were able to step forward and begin to fill their new responsibility for implementing their sections. As the new groups rolled into production the employees were able to step into their unique place in the organization. Unique roles and responsibilities is one of the key ingredients in building strong and healthy work teams. As the full implementation of the new lean focus ramped up, the pillar owners were each assigned the responsibility to ensure the entire plant population was fully informed on a regular basis.

Each pillar owner took a few minutes during the subsequent meetings to speak about the pillar they are leading. The pillar owners discussed the new responsibilities of their pillar, how the pillar would be organized, the policies of the new function and the ways in which the employee's responsibility would change as the new policies were implemented. Knowing what the future holds and how they fit in this future is one way in which anxiety is reduced. The employees would be affected by the activities within each pillar and as this information was shared, ambiguity was reduced allowing the employees to focus on fitting in with the new organization and implementing the changes in their daily work. The days moved on and the employees became comfortable with the new ways in which they would be expected to work and the new definition of success.

My role was announced, and I was the new safety pillar owner. Safety touches every aspect of manufacturing and affects the actions of all employees in every department. Ownership of this pillar gave me the opportunity to work with almost everyone in the plant. The first task I set for myself was to improve the lockout-tag out (LOTO) program for the plant. As I began my work within the new lean constraints I wanted to begin with something that would have an immediate impact on the way in which work got done, and one that would send the signal that people are important. One of the keys to the new lean environment is maintenance, and as I noted in the earlier discussion, will have an impact on the reduction of waste in lost hours and a direct personal effect on every employee. I felt this program was important because of the extensive maintenance work that would be performed in the autonomous maintenance pillar. All work within that pillar could put employees in harm's way without the means and understanding to render the equipment safe.

TRUST IS ESSENTIAL

Trust, as you know, covers three key elements in the work place. It is built through our personal growth as a child, and in the identification and evaluation of information that helps making a decision that someone or something is trustworthy. Ensuring our employees are safe, and that the safety program is equitably applied and repeatable across all organizations, would have a direct impact in rebuilding any damage to our trust relationship with our employees. The LOTO program assists the employees to work safely around the manufacturing equipment by creating guidelines for where to turn off power and eliminate the chance of accidental equipment starts during repair or cleaning. I wrote an outline for the LOTO program and detailed how the program would be written and how visual aids would be created. I submitted this outline to our corporate office and the senior leaders rolled it out at all 30 manufacturing facilities. That is how equity in program management is ensured. This gave me the opportunity to work with other safety pillar owners throughout the organization and begin building a strong working relationship across our functional groups. We worked together in building out a program that provided all of our employees greater safety. They appreciated the effort as it was a very visible display of our commitment to them.

The LOTO program I designed was uploaded to the safety pillar section of the lean shared folders on SharePoint for all plants to adopt and follow. SharePoint site is an Internet-based system with organized folders that employees can access from anywhere. With this, the programs were capable of being accessed from any person at any plant within the company, and allowed for easy sharing of best practices and kept all plants up to date with what was happening at all plants during the implementation. Information sharing is a key to helping an employee to make the decision to trust. Everything was shared openly with our employees to ensure they had all of the information they needed in rebuilding the trust relationship. We wanted them to feel like members of the team and thus become the evangelist in making the shift to lean.

With almost all change, there are bound to be problems. One of the most prevalent problems with the implementation of lean was how to keep the workforce motivated and engaged throughout the difficult and stressful period of change. Employees were performing their own jobs while taking on additional responsibilities for the implementation. They could see as they went through the process of learning that in many ways, when it was all complete and the changes were fully institutionalized, their own work would be very different. They could see the changes in how their jobs would be different after the implementation. This added stress made it difficult to keep employees on track. Everyone wanted to talk, and if they didn't have the information to share, then of course someone would try to fill in the blanks with rumor. The plant leadership struggled with this problem on a daily basis.

One of the most beneficial actions we took as a leadership team was to keep employees informed. We implemented a weekly update within each department and an overall plant update each month. The weekly updates were handled by each department head and could include face-to-face meetings and open discussion. We had all of the tools we needed including, as I noted earlier, SharePoint. We had email and snail mail at our disposal and could call for stand up meetings as necessary as long as the information continued to flow. I would gather my team on a weekly basis and discuss what we had completed so far toward the implementation, the next steps to be taken, and communicated where we were in relation to the implementation timeline. We continually discussed how the implementation affected the employees. We talked and talked until we had said everything there was to say, and then we began again from the beginning if needed until everyone had the message. Every meeting followed the same pattern. Pattern was important as it gave a sense that there was some stability in our little shaky world. Toward the end of each meeting, I opened it up to questions and of course the questions would always flow, and at times would cause us to start back at the beginning. This part of the meeting was most beneficial to maintaining the engagement of the employees. They often had questions that did not directly relate to the implementation, but the answers were necessary to building and strengthening our relationships and stressing the open communications. In a program as large and complex as lean implementation almost every aspect of the work life is affected by it. They were all very interested in how the company structure would look after everything was complete. Often times, there were questions I could not answer on the spot, so I told the team I would find the answer and provide it at the next meeting. We started the meetings with the answers to those questions. Giving this feedback, and getting the answers to those questions solidified their trust in me, and increased their engagement and commitment throughout implementation.

COMMUNICATE, COMMUNICATE, COMMUNICATE

The plant manager held the monthly meetings to cover and would cover all departments and processes to ensure he fully disclosed all aspects of the entire implementation. He was diligent in his preparations for the meeting to be sure to pass on any information from the leaders at the corporate office, and provided updates as best he could in regard to where each individual department was based on their timeline. Each pillar owner reported on what they were working on and gave information about how each pillar would affect the employees. They discussed the timeline and the next steps to be taken in their pillar. These meetings became familiar and provided the sense that the employees and managers were becoming a family. There was security in knowing that each month we would come together and in essence assess and celebrate our progress. After the information was passed to the employees, each department head gave an update on each department's level of implementation. This information was crucial to easing the fears of the employees and helping them to understand that the company would support and assist them through this period of change. It became acceptable again to trust as the information sharing increased employee engagement throughout the implementation.

Even in prosperous times, keeping a workforce engaged is challenging, and at times even more challenging than one would expect as the prosperity will likely reduce the urgency to be different (Catteeuw, 2007). Employees will always want to understand how they personally will be impacted, what is expected of them, and how they will benefit from the change taking place within the organization. Making it personal as we did in this study made all the difference in getting the hard work done. As Maslow noted so many years ago when writing what we now know as Maslow's Hierarchy of Needs, the threat at any level reduces the employees focus to resolving the threat before they can focus their attentions at the higher level needs such as an employer expects in a work environment. As they become comfortable with the changes and the way in which they fit in with the new team they begin to seek the personal benefit in the situation. It is human nature to expect something in return for your actions, so when employees are asked to increase their productivity and personal performance, it is only natural for them to wonder what's in it for them. We as managers have to be prepared to express the benefits in a way that is both personal and relevant, and if these answers aren't readily available everyone will notice. Not knowing impedes their commitment, engagement, and performance. Communication is everything and over communicating is not possible. At any point in your implementation you start to feel as though you have communicated enough, it is time to redouble your efforts. Employees satisfied with management communication during change have a more positive state of mind about the change and have more confidence in a successful change (Nelissen and Selm, 2008). Change is stressful, and not knowing what to expect during change causes more stress. Stress makes it difficult for employees to perform at their best. Communication eases the stress due to the unknown. Without the added stress of the unknown, the employee can focus on overcoming the normal difficulties that come with all change.

Bibliography

Abernethy, K., Piegari, G., and Reichgelt, H. (2007). Teaching project management: An experiential approach. *Journal of Computing Sciences in Colleges*, 22(3), 198–205. Retrieved from http://www.acm.org.

ADail. (April 1, 2013). Great leaders create superior organizational culture: Here's how. *Leadership Success*. [online blog]. Retrieved from http://www.leadershipsuccessnow.com/great-leaders-create-superior-organizational-culture-heres-how.

Ahuja, J. (2010). A study of virtuality impact on team performance. *The IUP Journal of Management Research*, 9(5), 27–56. Retrieved from http://proquest.umi.com.

Ambler and Associates. (February 27, 2014). *Communication on agile software projects*. [online]. Retrieved from http://www.agilemodeling.com.

American Society for Training and Development. (2008). *10 Steps to Successful Facilitation*. Danvers, MA: ASTD Press.

Anantatmula, V. and Thomas, M. (2010). Managing global projects: A structured approach for better performance. *Project Management Journal*, 41(2), 60–72. doi: 10.1002/pmj.20168.

Andres, H.P. (2002). A comparison of face-to-face and virtual software development teams. *Team Performance Management: An International Journal*, 8(1/2), 39–48. Retrieved from http://www2.hawaii.edu

Ardichvili, A., Page, V., and Wentling, T. (2003). Motivation and barriers to participation in virtual knowledge-sharing communities of practice. *Journal of Knowledge Management*, 7(1), 64. Retrieved from http://elearning.ice.ntnu.edu.

Berman, S. (2010). *Capitalizing on Complexity*. Somers, NY: IBM Global Business Services.

Bersin, J. (2012). It's not the CEO, it's the leadership strategy that matters. *Forbes*. [online]. Retrieved from www.forbes.com.

Bhasin, S. (2012). An appropriate change strategy for lean success. *Management Decision*, 50(3), 439–58. doi: 10.1108/00251741211216223.

Bjørn, P. and Ngwenyama, O. (2008). Virtual team collaboration: Building shared meaning, resolving breakdowns and creating translucence. *Information Systems Journal*, 19(3), 227–53. doi: 10.1111/j.1365-2575.2007.00281.x.

Blaskova, M. (2009). Correlations between the increase in motivation and increase in quality. *E+M Ekonomie a Management*, 4, 54. Retrieved from www. em.kbbarko.cz.

Boehm, B. and Turner, R. (2003). *Balancing Agility and Discipline: A Guide for the Perplexed*. Upper Saddle River, NJ: Addison-Wesley Professional.

Camacho, L.M. and Paulus, P.B. (1995). The role of social anxiousness in group brainstorming. *Journal of Personality and Social Psychology*, 68(6), 1071. Retrieved from http://psycnet.apa.org.

Carroll, J. (1995). The application of total quality management to software development. *Information Technology & People*, 8(4), 35. Retrieved from http://www.itandpeople.org.

Carter, C. (September 4, 2013). Could dressing like the boss lead to a promotion? *The Telegraph*. Retrieved from www.telegraph.co.uk.

Catteeuw, F. (2007). Employee engagement: Boosting productivity in turbulent times. *Organization Development Journal*, 25(2), 151–7. Retrieved from http://scholar.google.com/scholar?hl=en&btnG=Search&q=intitle:Employee+engagement:+Boosting+productivity+in+turbulent+times#0.

Chow, T. and Cao, D.B. (2008). A survey study of critical success factors in agile software projects. *Journal of Systems and Software*, 81(6), 961–71. doi: 10.1016/j.jss.2007.08.020.

Cockburn, A. (2009). *"I come to bury agile, not to praise it": Effective software development in the 21st century*. [online]. Retrieved from http://alistair.cockburn.us.

Dando, E. (August 2, 2013). Does your agile team have a bad apple? *Agile IQ Blog*. [online]. Retrieved from www.solutionsiq.com.

DeRosa, D.M., Hantula, D.A., Kock, N., and D'Arcy, J. (2004). Trust and leadership in virtual teamwork: A media naturalness perspective. *Human Resources Management*, 43(2), 219–32. Retrieved from http://www.wiley.com.

Duarte, D.L. and Snyder, N.T. (2006). Critical success factors. *Mastering Virtual Teams: Strategies, Tools, and Techniques that Succeed*. [online Google Books]. Retrieved from http://static.managementboek.nl.

The Economist Intelligence Unit. (2009). Organizational agility: How business can survive and thrive in turbulent times. *The Economist*. [online]. Retrieved from www.emc.com.

Elving, W.J.L. (2005). The role of communication in organisational change. *Corporate Communications*, 10(2), 129. Retrieved from http://www.corp commsmagazine.co.uk.

Fabiansson, C. (2007). Young people's perception of being safe globally and locally. *Social Indicators Research*, 80, 31–49. doi: 10.1007/s11205-006-9020-3.

Faircloth, B.S. and Hamm, J.V. (2005). Sense of belonging among high school students representing 4 ethnic groups. *Journal of Youth and Adolescence*, 34(4), 293–309. doi: 10.1007/s10964-005-5752-7.

Felps, W., Mitchell, T.R., and Byington, E. (2006). How, when, and why bad apples spoil the barrel: Negative group members and dysfunctional groups. *Research in Organizational Behavior*, 27, 175–222. Retrieved from www.elsevier.com.

Foundation for Critical Thinking. (2007). *To analyze thinking we must identify we must identify and question its elemental structures*. Retrieved from http://www.criticalthinking.org.

Forrester, W. S. (2010). Creating a customer communication strategy for ATIO (Pty) Ltd. Retrieved from http://umkn-dsp01.unisa.ac.za/handle/10500/3989.

Fowler, M. (February 2014). Application Architecture. [web blog series]. Retrieved from http://martinfowler.com/tags/application%20architecture.html.

Gassman, O. and von Zedtwitz, M. (2003). Trends and determinants of managing virtual R&D teams. *R&D Management*, 33(3), 243–62. Retrieved from doi: 10.1111/1467-9310.00296.

Glen, P. (2003). *Leading Geeks: How to Manage and Lead People Who Deliver Technology*. San Francisco, CA: Jossey-Bass.

Global CEO Survey. (2013). *PWC*. Retrieved from www.pwc.com.

Gokhale, A.A. (1995). Collaborative learning enhances critical thinking. *Journal of Technology Education*. Retrieved from http://scholar.lib.vt.edu.

Hale, R. (2000). The science of mentoring at Scottish hydro-electric. *Human Resource Management International Digest*, 8(7), 31. Abstract retrieved from http://www.emeraldinsight.com.

Halgin, D. (2009). What can managers learn from college basketball. *MITSloan Management Review*, 50(3). Retrieved from http://sloanreview.mit.edu.

Hambley, L.A., O'Neill, T.A., and Kline, T.J. (2007). Virtual team leadership: The effects of leadership style and communication medium on team interaction styles and outcomes. *Organizational Behavior and Human Decision Processes*, 103(1), 1–20.

Hasle, P., Bojesen, A., Jensen, P.L., and Bramming, P. (2012). Lean and the working environment: A review of the literature. *International Journal of Operations & Production Management*, 32(7), 829–49. doi: 10.1108/01443571211250103.

Hertel, G., Geister, S., and Konradt, U. (2005). Managing virtual teams: A review of current empirical research. *Human Resource Management Review*, 15(1), 69–95.

Herzberg, F. (1965). The new industrial psychology. *Industrial & Labor Relations Review*, 18(3), 364. Retrieved from http://www.ilr.cornell.edu/depts/ilrrev.

Highsmith, J. (2013). *Adaptive Leadership: Accelerating Enterprise Agility*. Upper Saddle River, NJ: Addison-Wesley.

Holton, J.A. (2001). Building trust and collaboration in a virtual team. *Team Performance Management*, 7(3), 36–47. Retrieved from www.emeraldinsight.com.

Hugos, M.H. (2009). *Business Agility: Sustainable Prosperity in a Relentlessly Competitive World* (vol. 12). Hoboken, NJ: John Wiley and Sons.

Johnson, M. (July 26, 2013). Top CIOs embrace the need for speed. *CIO*. Retrieved from www.cio.com.

Joseph, C. (February 13, 2014). Why is positive reinforcement important in the workplace? *Chron.* [online]. Retrieved from www.chron.com.

Kane-Urrabazo, C. (2006). Management's role in shaping organizational culture. *Journal of Nursing Management*, 14(3), 188–94. doi: 10.1111/j.1365-2934.2006.00590.x.

Kanter, R.M. (1968). Commitment and social organization: A study of commitment mechanisms in utopian communities. *American Sociological Review*, 33(4), 499–517. Retrieved from http://www.asanet.org.

Karpiscak, J. (2007). The effects of new technologies on the performance of virtual teams. Doctoral dissertation, Capella University, Minneapolis, Minnesota. Retrieved from ProQuest Dissertations and Theses database.

Kerth, N. (2013). *Project Retrospectives: A Handbook for Team Reviews*. Upper Saddle River, NJ: Addison-Wesley.

Kruchten, P. (2007). Voyage in the agile memeplex. *Queue*, 5(5), 1. doi: 10. 1145/1281881.1281893.

Larman, C. and Vodde, B. (2008). *Scaling Lean and Agile Development: Thinking and Organizational Tools for Large-Scale Scrum*. Upper Saddle River, NJ: Addison-Wesley.

Leffingwell, D. (2013). *Scaled agile framework*. [online]. Retrieved from www. scaledagileframework.com.

Lipponen, J., Olkkonen, M.-E. and Myyry, L. (2004). Personal value orientation as a moderator in the relationships between perceived organizational justice and its hypothesized consequences. *Social Justice Research*, 17(3), 275–92. Retrieved from http://www.springer.com.

Liu, X. and Batt, R. (2010). How supervisors influence performance: A multilevel study of coaching and group management in technology-mediated services. *Personnel Psychology*, 63(2), 265. Retrieved from http://www.wiley.com.

McCrimmon, M. (2010). A new role for management in today's post-industrial organization. *Ivey Business Journal*. [online]. Retrieved from http://www.iveybusinessjournal.com/topics/leadership/a-new-role-for-management-in-today's-post-industrial-organization#.UVWGk7_HOfQ.

Maslow, A.H. (1948). Some theoretical consequences of basic need-gratification. *Journal of Personality*, June, 402–416. doi: 10.1111/j.1467-6494.1948.tb02296.x.

May, A. and Carter, C. (2000). A case study of virtual team working in the European automotive industry. *International journal of Industrial Ergonomics*, 27(3), 171–86. Retrieved from http://www.sciencedirect.com.

Millward, L.J., Haslam, S.A., and Postmes, T. (2007). Putting employees in their place: The impact of hot desking on organizational and team identification. *Organization Science*, 18(4), 547–59. Retrieved from http://orgsci.journal.informs.org.

Mizrachi, N., Drori, I. and Anspach, R.R. (2007). Repertoires of trust: The practice of trust in multinational organization amid political conflict. *American Sociological Review*, 72(1), 143–65. Retrieved from http://www.asanet.org.

Moore, T.G. Jr. (2007). Virtual team member motivation in new product development: An investigation into the influence of leadership behaviors. Doctoral dissertation, Capella University, Minneapolis, Minnesota. Retrieved from ProQuest Dissertations and Theses database.

Murphey, P. (January 30, 2012). Revamp your organization for agile and lean. *Forester*. [online blog]. Retrieved from www.forester.com.

Näslund, D. (2008). Lean, six sigma and lean sigma: Fads or real process improvement methods? *Business Process Management Journal*, 14(3), 269–87. doi: 10.1108/14637150810876634.

Nee, Y.N. (2013). *What managers can do to support agile transformation*. Retrieved from www.infoq.com.

Nelissen, P. and Selm, M. Van. (2008). Surviving organizational change: How management communication helps balance mixed feelings. *Corporate*

Communications: An International Journal, 13(3), 306–18. doi: 10.1108/135 63280810893670.

Park, S., Henkin, A.B. and Egley, R. (2005). Teach team commitment, teamwork and trust: Exploring associations. *Journal of Educational Administration*, 43(4/5), 462. Retrieved from http://www.emeraldinsight.com.

Peskin, M. P. and Hart, J. (1996). Measuring the quality of computer systems development. *Benchmarking for Quality Management & Technology*, 3(2), 68. Retrieved from http://www.emeraldinsight.com.

Peters, L.M., and Manz, C.C. (2007). Identifying antecedents of virtual team collaboration. *Team Performance Management*, 13(3/4), 117–29.

Porter, M.E. (2008). *Competitive Advantage: Creating and Sustaining Superior Performance*. New York, NY: Simon & Schuster.

Porter, M.E. and Millar, V.E. (1985). How information gives you competitive advantage. *Harvard Business Review*. Retrieved from www.hbr.com.

Powell, A.L. (2000). Antecedents and outcomes of team commitment in a global, virtual environment. Doctoral dissertation, Indiana University, Indiana.

Rotter, J.B. (1971). Generalized expectancies for interpersonal trust. *American Psychologist*, 26(5), 443–52. Retrieved from http:// http://www.apa.org.

Ryan, A.M. and Kossek, E.E. (2008). Work-life policy implementation, breaking down or creating barriers to inclusiveness. *Human Resource Management*, 47(2), 296–310. Retrieved from http://ellenkossek.lir.msu.edu/ documents/07HRM47_2ryan.pdf.

Sarker, S., Valacich, J.S. and Sarker, S. (2003). Virtual team trust: Instrument development and validation in an IS educational environment. *Information Resources Management Journal*, 16(2), 35. Retrieved from http://igi-global.com.

Schwarz, G.M. and Watson, B.M. (2005). The influence of perceptions of social identity on information technology-enabled change. *Group & Organization Management*, 30(3), 289. doi: 10.1177/1059601104267622.

Shaughnessy, H. (January 1, 2013). The rise of lean and why it matters. *Forbes*. [online blog]. Retrieved from www.forbes.com.

Shenhar, A.J. and Dvir, D. (2007). *Reinventing Project Management: The Diamond Approach to Successful Growth and Innovation*. Boston, MA: Harvard Business Press.

Spillane, J.P. (2005). Distributed leadership. *The Educational Forum*, 69(2), 143–50. doi: 10.1080/00131720508984678.

Sternberg, R.J. and Grigorenko, E. (1993). Shared mental models in expert team decision making. In N.J. Castellan, Jr. (ed.), *Individual and Group Decision Making* (221–230). Hillsdale, NJ: Lawrence Erlbaum Associates, Inc. Retrieved from http://books.google.com.

Stone, A.G., Russell, R.F., and Patterson, K. (2004). Transformational versus servant leadership: A difference in leader focus. *Leadership & Organization Development Journal*, 25(4), 349–61. doi: 10.1108/01437730410538671.

Tuckman, B.W. (1965). Developmental sequence in small groups. *Psychological Bulletin*, 63(6), 384. doi: 10.1037/h0022100.

Turner, J.C. (1999). Some current issues in research on social identity and self-categorization theories. In N. Ellemers, R. Spears, and B. Doosje (eds), *Social Identity* (6–34). Malden, MA: Blackwell Publishers, Inc. [online Google books]. Retrieved from http://books.google.com.

VersionOne. (2013). *7th annual state of agile development survey*. [online]. Retrieved from www.versionone.com.

Ward, J. and Peppard, J. (2002). *Strategic Planning for Information Systems* (3rd edn). New York: John Wiley & Sons.

Weems-Landingham, V. 2004. The role of project manager and team member knowledge, skills and abilities (KSAs) in distinguishing virtual project team performance outcomes. Doctoral dissertation, Capella University, Minneapolis, Minnesota.

Weil, P. (2006). *The agility paradox*. Prepared for the CIO Summit, June 2006, in Cambridge, MA. Retrieved from http://ebusiness.mit.edu.

Weyuker, E.J., Ostrand, T.J., Brophy, J., and Prasad, R. (2000). Clearing a career path for software testers. *IEEE Software*, 17(2), 76. doi: 10.1109/52.841696.

Whetten, D.A. and Cameron, K.S. (1995). *Developing Management Skills* (3rd edn). New York: HarperCollins College Publishers.

Wilson, S. (2011). *Agile success rates*. June 2011. [online] Retrieved from www.agileoperations.net.

Winer, M.B. (1994). *Collaboration Handbook: Creating, Sustaining, and Enjoying the Journey* (1st edn). St. Paul, MN: Amherst H. Wilder Foundation.

Wise, T.P. (2011). Project team socialization: Are text messaging and IM damaging team performance? *The Journal for Quality and Participation*. 34(1). [online].

Wise, T.P. (2012). The effect of geographical separation, mediated communications, and culture on tester team member trust of other information technology virtual project team members. Doctoral dissertation in preparation, Capella University, Minneapolis, Minnesota.

Wise, T.P. (2013). *Trust in Virtual Teams: Organization, Strategies, and Assurance for Successful Projects*. Farnham: Gower Publishing Limited.

Wong, S-S. and Burton, R.M. (2000). Virtual teams: What are their characteristics, and impact on team performance? *Computational & Mathematical Organization Theory*, 6(4), 339–60. Retrieved from http://springer.com.

Zand, D.E. (1972). Trust and managerial problem solving. *Administrative Science Quarterly*, 17(2), 229–39. Retrieved from http://www.johnson.cornell.edu.

Zigurs, I. (2003). Leadership in virtual teams: Oxymoron or opportunity?. *Organizational dynamics*, 31(4), 339–51. Retrieved from http://www.journals.elsevier.com.

Index

acetylene gas balloons, 157
adaptability, dimensions of, 39, 42
adaptive teams, 40
agile, 2, 41, 98, 101–2, 139, 143
    approaches, 30
    assessment, 97
    backlog, 86
    basics, 40
    behaviors, 73, 134, 141
    categories, 97
    coaches, 1, 27, 73
    community, 40
    concepts, 23
    delivery, 22, 101, 139
    development, 5, 17, 50, 52
        focus, 43
        methods, 40, 50
    engineering methods, 73
    firms, 23, 44
    framework, 6, 97, 102, 143
        categories, 144
        well-defined, 103
    heat map, 103
    implementation strategies, 112
    methodologists, 44
    methods, 10–12, 15, 17–18, 20, 22–3,
        25, 28, 32, 45–7, 49–50, 80, 83,
        95, 111, 140, 144, 155
    model, 24
        best scalable, 6
        effective, 24
    paradigm, 24
    planning, 51
    practices, 10, 24, 103
    practitioners, 51
    processes, 10, 18, 26, 36, 40, 42, 49,
        51, 102, 134, 143
    programming techniques, 29
    project successes, 129
    teams, 6, 11, 17, 40, 73, 82–83, 89,
        91, 93–5, 97, 111, 136
    transformation processes, 24, 91,
        96, 99
'Agile Release Train' model, 6
Agile Software Development, 47–8
agility, 10, 12, 23, 26, 28, 36–7, 39, 44–6,
    51, 53, 60, 64, 79–80, 82, 86, 89,
    93, 95
    benefits of, 26
    effectiveness of, 55
    extending of, 22
    of governance processes, 102, 143
    and the implementation of
        software, 24
    organizational, 23, 44
ambiguity, 23–4, 60, 65–6, 76, 123, 159
    high, 25
    managing of, 77
American manufacturing
    environments, 151
American Society for Training and
    Development, 65
architectural team members, 89
architecture, 37, 39–41, 50, 52
    adaptive, 42
    antiquated, 40
    product, 41
    software, 17

well-defined, 52
Ardichvili, A., 123, 127
assessment, 5, 56, 60, 71, 82, 95, 97, 100, 130, 140
    analysis, 35, 132
    behavioral based, 140
    process, 82, 140
    questions, 100
attributes, 12, 25, 38–9, 68, 71, 121
authorities, 76–7, 85, 90
automation, 34, 43, 73, 97, 99, 144
    software, 56
    and tools, 87, 99, 103
autonomous maintenance, 151, 155, 157, 160
autonomy, 10, 12, 117, 125–6
    personal, 83
    team, 116, 118

behaviors, 1–2, 4, 12, 54–6, 59–63, 66, 69–70, 74, 77, 85, 97, 111, 121, 126, 134–8, 140–41, 144–5, 155
    agile, 73, 134, 141
    entrepreneurial, 155
    individual, 2, 53, 55, 77
    negative, 137
    new, 3, 75, 97, 128, 144, 151
    organizational, 11, 73
    poor, 60, 134–36, 138
    reinforced, 73
    team, 97
    transactional, 117
    trusting, 127
benefits, 2, 17, 26, 33, 96, 106, 136, 162
    of agility, 26
    desired, 45
    maximizing of, 33
    personal, 162
Berman, S., 22–3
best practices, implementation of, 157, 160

Blaskova, M., 115
BPM, 12, 16, 26, 47, 148
business agility, 20–21
business analysts, 81, 89
businesses, 6, 13, 15, 19–27, 37, 42, 46, 53, 73–74, 96, 139
    copying successful solutions from other, 13
    and information technology organizations, 46
    thriving on rumors, 72
    transformation of, 22
business goals, 2, 26
business information, 45
business leaders, 19–20, 47
business processes, 19, 22, 25–6, 45
business process management see BPM
Business Process Trends website, 35
business strategies, 6, 46, 56
business team members, 91
business values, 38

Cameron, K.S., 112, 114
Cao, D.B., 10
Capitalizing on Complexity, 22
Carnegie Mellon Software Engineering Institute Capability Maturity Model see CMMi
Carroll, J., 47
Carter, C., 126–27, 134
'catastrophic cliff dives,' 2, 26–7, 30
categories, 18, 97, 121, 141, 144
    agile, 97
    behavioral, 98–9
    high level, 141
    lean, 141–2
Catteeuw, F., 162
CEOs, 22–3, 30, 44–5, 56, 70
change agents, 45, 75

change management, 100, 129, 149–50,
        152, 155
chief executive officers, *see* CEOs
chief information officers, *see* CIOs
chief technology officers *see* CTOs
Chow, T., 10
CIOs, 26–7, 31–32, 44, 46, 61–2
CMMi, 95
cognitive-based trust, 68
collaboration, 25, 47, 50, 87–91, 109,
        118, 122, 126
    informal, 49
    planning, 89
    processes, 47
    and process management, 47–50
    teams, 89, 118, 127
    virtual team, 118
commitment, 10, 61, 69, 112, 121,
        124–5, 135, 150–51, 153–4, 158,
        160–62
    levels of, 151–4, 158
    management, 5
    team members, 64
communications, 3, 10, 12, 25, 45, 47–
        51, 53, 62, 68, 76, 83, 91, 108–9,
        119–20, 127, 135, 156, 162–3
    capabilities, 12, 45
    cross-cultural, 121
    devices, 120
    direct, 118
    face-to-face, 51, 119
    group, 121
    interventions, 118
    management, 163
    missed, 67
    one-way, 48
    open, 68, 161
    paired, 48
    platforms, 25
    providers, 32
    rich, 48–49

successful, 155
technological, 81
companies, 5, 10–11, 18–22, 25–8, 38,
        41, 43–6, 63–4, 69, 72, 115–16,
        119, 121, 124, 149–55, 158, 160,
        162
    agile, 24
    culture, 124, 157
    hierarchy of, 119
    information technology
        departments, 46
    pharmaceutical, 34
    policies of, 120
    startup, 41
    structure, 119, 161
competencies, 23, 44, 59, 121; *see also*
        management competencies
competition, 55–56, 147, 153
    heating up of, 30
    levels of, 31, 117
compliance, 17, 30, 57, 133, 148
    cursory, 134
    expected, 76
    lack-luster reinforcement, 133
    process, 95–100
conflicts, 7, 11, 62, 66–7, 118, 127, 130,
        149
continuous process improvement,
        156
core competency, 22–4, 44, 121
costs, 15, 17–18, 22, 27, 33, 41, 50, 96,
        132, 147
    high, 16
    minimal monthly, 124
    operating, 147
    reduction of, 18, 26
co-workers, 72–73, 136
creativity, 12, 15, 56, 93, 115–18, 137
cross-functional improvements, 29
CTOs, 61–62
cultural awareness, 120, 123–4

culture, 5, 10, 12, 24, 53, 55–6, 60, 62–4,
        77, 107, 109, 119, 121, 123–4,
        129, 157
    company, 124, 157
    of continuous improvements, 5
    of creativity, 56
    desired, 56
    individual, 124
    multiple, 119
    of openness, 55
    organizational, 62, 104, 118, 123
    of rapid delivery, 56
    risk-averse, 24, 45
customer-business relationships, 108
customer experiences, 6, 31
customer feedback, 82
customer requirements, 36
customer service organizations, 31
customer transactions, 24
customer values, 6, 21, 30–32, 139
    calculating of, 32
    defining of, 32, 32–4
    modeling of, 30
cycle, 25–6, 40, 101, 139, 141
    product delivery, 22
    regular release, 42
    two-week production, 111

Dando, E., 136, 138
decision-making, internal, 24
decisions, 11, 29, 41, 65–6, 69, 71–2,
        74–5, 77, 81, 93, 103, 118–19,
        126, 131, 135, 140, 148–9, 160
    cognitive, 69
    dumb, 157
    equitable management policy, 111
    fact-based, 158
    independent, 126
    leadership style, 117
    manufacturing, 149
    technology, 122, 126

defect tracking, 98
department directors, 59; see also
        directors
department heads, 158, 161–2
dependencies, 66
    contrived, 125
    interaction of, 64, 67
    project, 61, 76
    reciprocation of, 64, 68
    well-defined, 52
developers, 10–11, 50, 53, 79–81, 88,
        105, 111
    groups of, 81
    software, 16
    strong, 11
    systems, 109
    tools, 73
development organizations, 10, 47, 79
development team members, 73
directors, 54, 58, 60, 75–6, 132–4, 144
    department, 59
    group, 75
    organization, 60
distribution processes, 89–90
Divr, D., 113
documentation, 49–51, 85, 147, 157
dollars, 26–8, 31, 34, 46, 115
Drucker, Peter, 52
Duarte, D.L., 109, 121, 125–7
duties, 45, 63, 65–6

education, 55
employee groups, 122
employees, 18, 20–21, 28–31, 58, 60,
        63–4, 68–77, 79, 82–4, 104–5,
        110–12, 114–16, 121, 123–5, 129,
        133, 145, 148–63
    empowering of, 75, 77
    engagement, 31, 81, 127
    focus, 162
    full-time, 59

good, 153
hourly, 150
individual, 5
long-time, 157
loyalties, 82–6, 91
new, 58, 153
secrecy of, 159
underperforming, 60
employers, 70, 162
empowerment, 2, 73–6, 93, 110
engagement, rules of, 84, 161–2
engineering life cycle, 61, 141
enterprise processes, 97, 102, 143–4
entrepreneurial behaviors, 155
environment, 7, 12, 23, 46, 62–3, 71,
    74, 76–7, 79, 81–2, 84, 91, 110,
    115–16, 119, 123–5, 151, 154–5
agile, 93, 111
changing, 22, 44
collaborative, 87, 119, 121
corporate, 12, 47
homogeneous, 109
lean, 88, 138, 153, 159
new, 11, 149
regulatory, 43
team, 82, 86, 130, 136
equipment, 57, 85, 147, 156–8, 160
efficiency of, 157
manufacturing, 160
reactor safety, 71
executive leaders, 76
executives, 1, 12, 19, 23–4, 29, 31, 44,
    53, 103, 117
external customer transactions, 24

facilitation, 49, 55, 74, 106, 121, 130;
    see also planning
failure rate, 10, 18–19, 156
familial relationships, 137
family, 83, 86, 112, 124, 162
family illnesses, 83

family membership, 137
family units, 86
fear, 11, 20, 45, 63, 70, 83, 86, 113, 116,
    145, 150, 152–5, 158, 162
of failure and the unknown, 150
organization, 150
wide-eyed, 152
feedback, 11, 27, 37, 39, 54, 125, 127,
    161
see also customer feedback
positive, 144
providing of, 116
Felps, W., 136–7
Four Quadrant Project Chartering
    Guide, 106–7
'Four Spheres of Model and Lean
    Transformation,' 1–2, 55, 62,
    67, 81, 87, 95, 100, 103, 109, 130,
    134, 140
Fowler, Martin, 41
freedom, 7, 10, 74–5, 77, 86–7, 93,
    110–12, 117, 140
levels of, 82, 118
maximum, 63, 93
technological, 123
functions, 16, 19, 30, 45–7, 88, 112–13,
    144
dependent, 151
heavy, 147
new, 159
quality program, 132

gas balloons, 157
Gates, Bill, 56
Global CEO Survey, 44–45
goals, 24–6, 28–30, 32, 34, 55–8, 60,
    66–8, 73–4, 76–77, 81–2, 84, 91,
    93, 95, 98, 100, 124–6, 130
common, 66
common project, 6, 28, 30, 116
departmental, 45

engineering, 58
individual team, 125
longer-term, 91
organizational, 18, 34–5, 55
primary, 42
quantitative, 26
shared, 158
SMART, 52
target, 18, 27, 29, 32
technical, 57
test organization, 99
Google, 13, 15–16
governance, 93, 104, 109, 127
    levels of, 127
    management, 2–3, 93–128, 150
    processes, 29, 94, 102, 107–8, 143
    programs, 29
    of project selection, 30, 98
group communications, 121
group directors, 75
group members, 65–6, 130–31
groups, 11, 13, 56–7, 59, 62, 65–6, 69,
        71, 75, 81, 110–11, 117, 119,
        121–2, 124, 126, 130–31, 136
    employee, 122
    functional, 160
    independent, 81
    major, 62
    new, 159
    project, 95
    software delivery, 23
    and teams, 65–7

Hambley, L.A., 117
hardware, 25, 56–8, 62
    computer, 113
    installers, 58
    underutilized, 62
heat maps, 100, 102–3, 106–7, 144
Herzberg, F., 114, 121, 123, 125
high level categories, 141

Hill, Sam, 4
Hugos, Michael, 21
human resource, 30, 111, 154
    managers, 114
    policies, 93, 109–12, 123
    practices, 110
    strategies, 112
    variables, 112

implementation, 1–2, 10, 17–19, 29,
        32, 35, 49, 100, 104–5, 129,
        150–51, 154–5, 157–62
    approaches, 32
    effective, 100
    failed, 19
    plans, 158
    processes, 129, 133, 159
    strategies, 7, 18–20, 105
    successful, 20, 123, 155, 158
    teams, 122
    timeline, 161
improvement and short feedback
        loops, 51
IM systems, 12, 50, 62, 119–20
individual behaviors, 2, 53, 55, 77
industrial environment, 79; see also
        environment
informal collaborations between
        system stakeholders, 49
information, 15, 17, 20–22, 45–7, 49–50,
        67–72, 76, 81, 84–5, 87, 103, 108,
        114, 125–27, 136, 158–62
    gaps, 71–72
    projects, 17, 125
    sharing of, 71, 73, 158
    silo-based, 45
    systems, 46, 110
    technology teams, 21, 46, 147
information systems and information
        technology see IS/IT
instant messaging see IM

institutional-based trust, 68
internal assessments, 59, 95
internal decision-making, 24
internet, 71–72, 160
internet age, 15
internet surfers, 16
investment models, 33
investment priorities, 6
investments, 7, 26–7, 29, 34, 36, 41, 72
investment themes, 6
IS/IT, 46
    delivery processes, 47
    strategies, 46
    systems, 47
IT delivery process, 46–7
iterations, 6, 51–2
    earlier, 38
    time-boxed, 6
iterative development methods, 19
iterative development processes, 10

Japanese business philosophy
        of continuous process
        improvement, 156
jargon, 3–4
Jensen, P.L., 148
jobs, 62, 125, 148, 153, 158, 161
    with advancement opportunities,
        136
    assignments, 148
    high profile, 136
    rotation, 124
    traditional roles, 149
jobs experiences, 121
Johnson, M., 24
joint venture companies, 56
Joseph, C., 144

Kaizen, 107, 156
Kanban, 17, 40
Kano model, 38

Kanter, R.M., 121
Karpiscak, J., 127
Kentucky Derby, 55
Kerth, N., 52
Kline, T.J., 117
knowledge, 15, 20, 52, 58–9, 67–9, 81,
        86, 106–7, 112, 123, 127, 130,
        136, 149
    age, 44–5
    base, 20, 25, 79, 87, 95
    common, 50, 64
    distribution, 127
    essential, 64
    important, 50
    levels, 153
    management, 51
    processes, 45
    statistical, 156
    technical, 57
    tribal, 85, 107
    workers, 58
knowledge-sharing processes, 45
'known problems,' 106–7
'known solutions,' 106–7
Kock, N., 116
Kossek, E.E., 111, 123
Kotter, J. P., 6
Kranz, G., 74
Kruchten, P., 12, 46

languages, 4, 18, 24
    common, 3, 50
    multi-platform, 40–41
    specialized, 41
Larman, Craig, 5
leaders, 10–11, 25–26, 28, 45–7, 55–8,
        61–6, 69–70, 72–7, 79–81, 83–4,
        86, 103, 116–18, 133–5, 138,
        144–5, 147–8, 150–55
    distributed, 64
    guidelines for, 95

lower-level, 117
potential, 65
leadership, 10–13, 55, 60, 64, 66–8, 74,
        76, 103–5, 109–10, 113, 116–17,
        126, 130, 133, 135, 138, 145,
        148–9
    activities, 125
    changes, 27, 33
    competencies, 126
    confidence, 109
    diffused, 118–19
    distribution of, 64, 67
    executive, 147
    issues, 112, 116
    opportunities, 67, 116, 121
    organizational, 132
    perspectives, 84
    responsibilities, 48, 60, 119, 138
    roles, 11, 67, 69, 117
    skills, 11–12, 125
    strategies, 56, 82
    styles, 56, 58–9, 117–19
    stylizing of, 2, 55
    teams, 25, 29, 76, 103–4, 138, 161
    transformational, 10, 59–60, 63
lean adoptions, 18
lean behaviors, 135, 138, 141
lean categories, 141–42
lean environment, 88, 138, 153, 159
lean implementations, 1–2, 5–6, 15, 17,
        19, 21, 31, 95, 149, 154, 160–61
lean initiatives, 11, 26, 150
lean manufacturing, 147–53, 155, 157,
        159, 161, 163
lean methodologies, 1, 30, 106
lean methods, 3, 10, 15–16, 18, 20, 27,
        29, 31, 82, 86, 88, 97, 99–100,
        110, 129–30, 138, 140, 145
lean opportunities, 18, 34
lean organizations, 29, 97

lean practitioners, 10, 144
lean principles, 18
lean processes, 11, 26, 95, 100, 112
lean processing, 60, 75
lean process teams, 49
lean programs, 5, 53, 55, 103
lean projects, 30, 35, 77, 144
lean skills, 18
lean strategies, 95
lean teams, 30, 52–3, 74, 91, 138, 140–41
lean thinking, 5–7
lean tools, 5, 18
lean transition, 28–30, 52
Leffingwell, Dean, 6, 24
life cycle, 3, 15–17, 21, 24–8, 43, 49, 61,
        88, 94, 98–9, 125, 128, 140–41,
        147–8
logistics pillars, 157
LOTO program, 159–60
lower level managers, 44

management, 1–3, 5–6, 16–17, 23,
        25–6, 30, 42–44, 46–7, 63, 84–5,
        97–107, 109–13, 115–17, 121–3,
        127–9, 139–41, 148–50, 152–3
    business process, 12, 16, 26, 47, 148
    communications, 163
    competencies, 121
    governance, 2–3, 93–128, 150
    organizational, 68
    project, 23, 57, 101, 109, 127, 139
    questions, 140–41
    responsibilities, 149
    teams, 47, 60, 115, 117, 121, 153
managers, 10, 12, 53–4, 56, 59–61,
        63–4, 68–75, 79–80, 85–6, 106,
        112, 115–17, 120, 123–4, 132–3,
        149–50, 158, 162
    effective, 119, 121
    hard-working, 74

helping of, 11, 110, 116
human resource, 114
lower level, 44
plant, 158, 162
program, 25
project, 11, 23, 61, 100, 117
project information, 122
senior level, 84
of work teams, 120
manufacturing equipment, 160
Manz, C.C., 118
market value, 33
Maslow, A.H., 83, 113–14, 119, 123, 162
Maslow's Hierarchy, 83, 114, 116, 162
Massachusetts Institute of
    Technology *see* MIT
maturity, 65–6, 95–6, 103, 105
    improvement process, 95
    process, 82, 95
    team, 65–7
    understanding group, 65
meetings, 54–55, 58, 62, 72, 75, 86, 131,
        137, 150, 152, 155, 158–9, 161–2
    club, 65
    daily, 27
    director, 133
    face-to-face, 161
    monthly, 162
    one-on-one, 72
    planning, 51
    plant, 150, 158
    special, 25
MIT, 5, 23, 44
Mitchell, T.R., 136
Mizrachi, N., 120, 123
Moore, T.G., 118, 126
motivation, 63, 109–10, 112, 114, 119,
        125
motivational factors, 114–15
motivational opportunities, 116

motivational theories, 114–15
motivational tools, 118, 157

Näslund, D., 13
Nee, Y.N., 79
new employees, 58, 153
new groups pillars, 151
new team members, 84, 113
NTCP diamond analysis process, 113

online ‹dashboard,› 58, 116
operations teams, 42, 90
organizational behaviors, 11, 73
organizational changes, 144–5
organizational culture, 62, 104, 118,
        123
organizational ecosystems, 64, 86
organizational innovation processes,
        7, 149
organizational institutionalization,
        129–45
organizational leaders, 5, 17–18, 57,
        84, 150, 153, 155, 158
organizational objectives, 28
organizational plans, 155
organizational results, 53
organizational strategies, 95
organizational units, 24
organizational verticals, 127
organization directors, 60
organizations, 1–3, 13, 17–24, 27–36,
        44–7, 55–56, 58–60, 62–4, 73,
        82–85, 94–5, 105–8, 123–6,
        129–32, 140, 148–50, 152–5,
        158–60
    agile, 22, 135
    dependent, 124
    flexible, 59
    mature, 66
    multiple, 119

new, 105, 150–51, 158–9
respected, 107
successful, 10
virtual project, 121
Ostrand, T.J., 81

peer relationships, 127
Peppard, J., 46
peripheral processes, 25
personality-based trust, 68
Peters, L.M., 118
pillar owners, 159–60, 162
pillars, 151, 155, 157, 159–60, 162
    logistics, 157
    new groups, 151
    successful, 157
planning, 26, 35, 44, 47, 49–51, 58,
        60–61, 75, 82, 89, 94–5, 98, 111,
        122, 126, 133, 140
    agile, 51
    anti-static, 51
    daily, 51
    documents, 51
    meetings, 51
    project, 27, 110, 113
    sessions, 46
    strategic, 47, 95
plant leadership teams, 158
policies, 69, 72, 84, 110–12, 114, 120,
        123, 125, 159
    corporate, 123
    effective, 114
    new, 159
    open organizational, 123
    participative, 123
    and procedures, 120, 125
    work group, 124
    work-home life, 111
poor behaviors, 60, 134–6, 138
Porter, M.E., 30

Porter's value chain model, 30
problems, 9, 12–13, 19–20, 35–6, 45,
        50–52, 57–8, 64, 67, 80, 83, 85,
        103–5, 107, 116, 133, 138, 160–61
    facilitation of, 106
    network, 31
    technology, 11
problem-solving activities, 152
problem-solving initiatives, 11
problem-solving techniques, 103
process behaviors, 95–100
process compliance, 95–100
processes, 7, 9–11, 17–19, 21–2, 25–6,
        28, 40, 42–7, 49–50, 53–4, 58–60,
        94–102, 105, 109, 132–3, 139–40,
        142–4, 147–9
    business, 19, 22, 25–6, 45
    collaborative, 47
    enterprise, 97, 102, 143–4
    governance, 29, 94, 102, 107–8, 143
    knowledge-sharing, 45
    peripheral, 25
    strategic planning, 44, 46–7, 95
process improvements, 7, 11, 35, 106
process maturity, 82, 95
process teams, 95
process transformations, 96
product architecture, 41
product life cycles, 21, 43, 88, 140, 147
programs, 1, 3, 5, 30, 80, 90, 93, 95,
        123, 157, 159–61
    cohesive, 119
    comprehensive, 46, 61
    computer, 80
    job rotation, 125
    local on-site speaker's
        development, 116
    management, 160
    measurement, 138
    metrics, 61

problem-solving, 11
progressive training, 28
sponsors, 1
strategic, 5
project characteristics, 97, 103, 144
project charters, 77
project dependencies, 61, 76
project governance, 98
project groups, 95
project information, 17, 125
project leaders, 67, 113
project management, 23, 57, 101, 109,
        127, 139
project participants, 61–62, 67, 87
project planning, 27, 110, 113
projects, 11, 17–18, 23, 25–32, 46–8,
        50–52, 57–8, 61–2, 64, 67–9,
        76–77, 91, 100–106, 109–10, 113,
        117–20, 132–3, 143–5
    agile, 10, 17, 50–51, 103
    complex, 87, 94, 105
    controversial, 29
    corporate, 94
    information technology, 47
    interdependent, 17
    iterative, 97
    managing software, 17, 42
    multiple dependent, 94
    three-to-four-month, 41
    virtual, 67
project selection, 29–30, 35, 106
    governance of, 30, 98
    improvement, 35
    lean, 35
    process, 106
    process improvement, 35
project teams, 25, 35, 67, 76, 82, 88–9,
        94, 103, 109, 111–14, 118, 120,
        122, 132, 134, 141
project tracking, 105

project transparency, 68
publications, 6
    Agile Software Development, 47–8
    Balancing Agility and Discipline, 36
    Capitalizing on Complexity, 22
    The Economist, 24, 43–6
    Global CEO Survey, 44–5
    Scaling Lean and Agile Development,
        5
    Trust in Virtual Teams, 93

QA managers, 4
QMS, 84, 133
quality management system see QMS

relationships, 21, 53–4, 83, 89, 91,
        93, 101, 109–10, 118, 124, 158,
        160–61
    building of, 125
    customer-business, 108
    familial, 137
    peer, 127
    transactional, 81
    trust, 69
research, 23, 42, 44, 67
    effective, 46
    employee motivational, 115
    tools, 15
return on investment see ROI
reverse quality, concept of, 39
review processes, 85–6, 90
risk-averse culture, 24, 45
risks, 38, 74
roadmaps, 25, 27, 154
ROI, 26–7
rules of engagement, 84, 161–2

SAFe, 6, 24
safety, 83, 86–7, 114–15, 121, 124, 151,
        155, 157, 159

initiatives, 157
procedures, 157
programs, 160
standards, 157
safety pillar leaders, 157
Sarker, S., 123
scaled agile framework *see* SAFe
Scaling Lean and Agile Development, 5
'SE Based Team' (project), 102–3, 143
self-assessment, 35, 97, 132
senior leaders, roles of, 73, 135, 147,
       150, 152, 155, 158, 160
separation of responsibility, 126
Seven QC Tools (organization), 18, 107
SharePoint, 160–61
Shaughnessy, H., 18
Shenhar, A.J., 113
shift workers, 158
Sigma, 7, 16, 28, 96, 104, 106–7
   analysis, 7
   approaches, 6
   Black Belts, 16
   differentiated from Lean, 6
   Lean, 101, 139
   popularity, 16
   practitioners, 7, 16
   programs, 7
   strategies, 18
   tools, 156
Six Sigma, 6
skills, 3, 10–12, 17, 52, 55–6, 60, 64,
       66–8, 88, 91, 94, 109, 116, 121,
       127, 132, 135–7, 151
   augmentation of, 113
   development of, 11
   essential, 127
   individual, 3
   missing, 60
   new, 12, 60, 113, 116, 155
   well-developed, 59

well-shaped, 10
well-tuned, 65
SMART Goals, 52
SMEs, 106–7, 115
Snyder, N.T., 109, 121, 125–7
software architecture, 17
software developers, 16
software development life cycle *see*
   SDLC
software systems, 39
Spillane, J.P., 117
stakeholders, 36, 49–50, 75, 77, 135
strategic planning processes, 44, 46–7,
   95
strategies, 1, 13, 23, 41, 46, 49, 82, 87–8,
       95, 108–10, 120
   business, 6, 46, 56
   critical thinking, 148
   effective, 110
   implementation, 7, 18–20, 105
   integrated, 121
   leadership, 56, 82
   lean process, 95
   motivational, 123
   year-long, 95
styles, 56, 61–2, 66, 117–18
   'cowboy,' 51
   distracted communication, 55
   transactional management, 117
   transformational leadership, 117
subject matter experts *see* SMEs
substitution value, 33
success, 1–3, 10, 12–13, 20–23, 27, 31,
       47–9, 52, 57, 74, 77, 100, 123,
       126–7, 149, 151, 157, 159
   agile project, 129
   degrees of, 10, 13
   global, 23
   incremental, 10
   organizational, 155

personal, 26
potential team, 109, 112
rates, 10, 18
systems, 5, 46–7, 70, 80, 88–90, 105,
    127, 132
    developers, 109
    electronic financial, 61
    engineers, 81
    major back-office, 42
    multimillion-dollar end-to-end, 57
    socio-technical, 148
    software, 39

target goals, 18, 27, 29, 32
team autonomy, 116, 118
team behaviors, 97
team building, 64, 121
    effectiveness of, 89
    tools, 127
team dynamics, 12, 109–10, 116
    changes in, 137
    new, 109
team environment, 82, 86, 130, 136
team governance strategies, 2, 109
team leader and team member
    competency, 120–21
team leadership, 68, 85, 105, 110, 118,
    126
team maturity, 65–7
team members, 6, 11–12, 17, 25–8,
    49–50, 63–4, 66–75, 81–6, 88–90,
    93–4, 103–5, 111–12, 117–20,
    122, 125–7, 131–3, 135–8, 144–5
    architectural, 89
    business, 91
    development, 73
    new, 84, 113
    old, 73
    remote, 122
    virtual, 68–9, 122, 127

team membership, 17, 27, 82, 86
team roles, 2–3, 79–91, 149
teams, 2–6, 24–32, 48–9, 51, 57–60,
    62–3, 65–70, 73, 77, 81–91, 93–4,
    97–100, 102–8, 110–13, 115–24,
    126–7, 130–38, 142–5
    agile project, 25, 112
    autonomous, 37, 52
    collaboration, 118, 127
    combined project, 62
    cross-organizational, 55
    dispersed, 110, 122
    employee, 116
    engineering, 53–4, 56, 60, 62
    face-to-face project, 111
    high-performance, 12, 117
    lean, 30, 52–3, 74, 91, 138, 140–41
    lean methodology, 108
    lean project, 77
    lean transition, 29
    network, 31, 62
    new, 24, 84, 162
    product, 90
    project, 25, 35, 67, 76, 82, 88–9, 94,
        103, 109, 111–14, 118, 120, 122,
        132, 134, 141
    quality assurance, 133–4
    successful, 107
    test, 34, 57, 88, 98–9, 142
    traditional face-to-face, 116, 118
    twenty-first century project, 109
    virtual project, 12, 64, 93, 109–10,
        115–16, 125–6
teamwork, 55, 62–3, 69, 77, 109, 121
technology, 7, 21–5, 38, 45–6, 58, 62,
    80, 109, 113, 117–18, 122, 124,
    126, 132
    axis, 113
    changes, 42, 113
    choices, 126

decisions, 122, 126
expectations, 113
industries, 82
issues, 105
point-of-view, 36
problems, 11
processes, 7, 22
risks, 38, 74
skills, 12
teams, 12
video conference, 127
virtual, 12
workers, 7, 81, 113
television, 72
templates, 125, 132–34
  common work, 134
  necessary, 133
  new process, 132
  standard work, 125
  tracking, 133
testers, 10, 81, 86–90, 109
test management tools, 98–9
test teams, 34, 57, 88, 98–9, 142
Thomas, M., 109
Thomas P. Wise, 93
timelines, 50, 52, 62, 77, 111, 162
time zones, 11, 119–21
tools, 11–12, 16, 18, 45, 47, 51, 61, 97–9,
    102–5, 108, 112–13, 122–3, 126,
    130–31, 141, 143–4, 147, 149
  and automation, 87, 99, 103
  complex process improvement, 28
  decision support, 30
  defect management, 122
  developers, 73
  electronic communication
    mediation, 127
  multiple collection, 105
  organization changes, 105
  using search engine analysis, 16

total quality management see TQM
tracking templates, 133
training, 15–16, 25, 28, 55, 57, 82, 84,
    94, 97–9, 102–3, 107–9, 112–16,
    119, 124–5, 132, 141, 143–4,
    153–4
  classes, 29
  experience, 132
  exposure, 97
  guided, 125
  investment in, 26
  modules, 29, 132
  peer, 125
  sessions, 115
  skills, 116
transactional behaviors, 117
transactional leadership, 57, 63, 68,
    117
transactional relationships, 81
transformation, 4–6, 13, 21–2, 33–4,
    59, 64, 95, 99
  of businesses, 22
  efforts, 31–32
  initiatives, 19
  leaders, 117
  processes, 3
transition, 23, 26–7, 52, 73, 130, 145,
    148, 153
  budget, 27
  plans, 27
  process, 27, 144
  times, 147
trust, 10–12, 53–4, 64–5, 67–71, 73–4,
    77, 83, 86–8, 93–4, 109–10, 112,
    121, 124–7, 136, 155, 160–62
  bases of, 68
  building of, 2, 67, 69, 74, 120
  cognitive, 68–72, 94, 136
  cognitive-based, 68
  employee engendering, 121

healthy, 69
  institutional-based, 68
  personality-based, 68, 70
Trust in Virtual Teams, 93
trust relationships, 69
trustworthiness, 70–71
Two-Factor Theory, 114

value, 6, 17, 22, 30, 33–4, 40, 42, 60,
    71–2, 75
  customer, 6, 21, 30–32, 139
  definition of, 33
  intrinsic, 33
  market, 33
  substitution, 33
value chains, 30, 34
value creation, 20, 33
Value Stream Mapping
    (organization), 18
virtual project organization, 121
virtual project teams, 12, 64, 93,
    109–10, 115–16, 125–6
  collaboration, 118
  members, 68–9, 122, 127
vision, 3, 5, 25, 28–9, 55, 57–60, 63–4,
    74–7, 84, 89, 91, 119, 150, 152,
    154–5
  consistent, 154
  desired, 76
  leader's, 29
  new, 75
  personal, 75
  shared, 59
Vodde, Bas, 5
Voice of the Customers (organization),
    17–18
von Zedtwitz, M., 126

Ward, J., 46
waste reduction, 1, 18, 29, 31–2, 159

Weems-Landingham, V., 120
Welch, Jack, 56
Wentling, T., 123
Weyuker, E.J., 81
Whetten, D.A., 112, 114
whiteboard sessions, 48–50, 88
Wilson, S., 10
Winer, M.B., 91
wireless providers, 25
Wise, Michael P., 147–63
Wise, Thomas P., 93
work environments, 22, 117, 119, 162
  safe, 118
  virtual, 79, 123
workers, 7, 33–5, 84, 86, 115, 147
  assembly-line, 28
  poor, 135
  shift, 158
  skilled, 28
  technology, 7, 81, 113
workflows, 33–4, 90, 148
work folders, 133–34
workforce, 110, 116, 121, 161–2
work groups, 111, 124
work instructions and procedures,
    85, 157
workloads, 112, 137
workplace, 45, 86
work teams, 53, 75, 119–20, 122
  decentralized, 126
  effective, 120
  global, 125
  healthy, 159
  high performing lean, 54
  virtual, 125

Xtreme programming, 61

Zand, D.E., 121
Zigurs, I., 116

If you have found this book useful you may be interested in other titles from Gower

Business Leadership for IT Projects
Gary Lloyd
Hardback: 978-1-4094-5690-2
e-book PDF: 978-1-4094-5691-9
e-book ePUB: 978-1-4724-0811-2

Lean and Digitize
An Integrated Approach to Process Improvement
Bernardo Nicoletti
Hardback: 978-1-4094-4194-6
e-book PDF: 978-1-4094-4195-3
e-book ePUB: 978-1-4094-8464-6

Project Risk Governance
Managing Uncertainty and Creating Organisational Value
Dieter Fink
Hardback: 978-1-4724-1904-0
e-book PDF: 978-1-4724-1905-7
e-book ePUB: 978-1-4724-1906-4

Advances in Project Management
Narrated Journeys in Unchartered Territory
Edited by Darren Dalcher
Hardback: 978-1-4724-2912-4
e-book PDF: 978-1-4724-2913-1
e-book ePUB: 978-1-4724-2914-8

Business Architecture
A Practical Guide
Jonathan Whelan and Graham Meaden
Hardback: 978-1-4094-3859-5
e-book PDF: 978-1-4094-3860-1
e-book ePUB: 978-1-4094-6153-1

GOWER